Once Upon a Time Called COVID-19

"The Community of We" Part Two

(When God Allowed Me to Kill Myself)

Examine yourselves, whether ye be in the faith; prove your own selves. Know ye not your own selves, how that Jesus Christ is in you, except ye be reprobates?

2 Corinthians 13:5 KJV

Examine yourselves to see if your faith is genuine. Test yourselves. Surely you know that Jesus Christ is among you[a]; if not, you have failed the test of genuine faith.

2 Corinthians 13:5 NLT

Examine yourselves to see whether you are in the faith; test yourselves. Do you not realize that Christ Jesus is in you—unless, of course, you fail the test?

2 Corinthians 13:5 NI

Dedication

It should be a given fact that I am blessed to pen this offer back to the Lord along with any glory from it as a standing dedication. Yet, I also dedicate work to others as well. This one is bittersweet for me. I dedicate this musing to a dear friend and warrior whose memory and contact spanned most of our lives.

The very last conversation we shared was concerning faith, this work along with upcoming Congressional bills to assist veterans. I was prepared to call him and deliver some good news and extra nuggets of information on Monday. He passed suddenly on Saturday with me unexpectedly receiving the news on Sunday morning.

It was Curtis Anthony Jennings that said with his husky voice and piercing laugh, "That sounds like something we need to read! At least I do." So many things hindered the start and completion of this work. COVID-19 was only a part of it. Surgeries, car accidents with recovery (continuous) and rehabilitation from injuries and surgeries, many deaths with emotional draining of grief and just everyday life with new restrictions hindered me at various junctions. But the transition to the life of Curtis hit in a way that nothing else did. I dedicate this to our last conversation and the example of a true servant leader that was displayed with excellence in the Kingdom as well as the military.

In addition, my sister affectionately known as Teena changed her address to heaven. While I was wondering why I could not finish this manuscript, a truly short one at that, I discovered that it was to gather more information and to honor those who went on before us. Dedication and honoring those with literary works should be a norm for those of us who are inspired by the life of others. Whether close friends or blood relatives, we can never live this life alone and solitary. It took more than one person to give birth to us. And it will take more than one person to inspire us. Rest in peace. God is peace.

Introduction

During early 2020 there was a shift in American Society. Many things loomed on the horizon. We witnessed political upheavals as well as social unrest in many areas. But, between the race relations issues, constant military conflicts, economy and political wranglings, something crept into our lives and began to disrupt it all. So many people had prophetic "connections" into the year being a double number, vision being best at 20/20 and a host of other things. I told many that 20/20 only meant to me that I would see clearly what hit us. I kept sensing something hard brewing. Then suddenly it hit: COVID-19. All the prophetic wrangling came to a head and intermingled into the political realm. Now, everyone was divided as they were during political campaigns. Death covered the earth in such a way as to elicit fear among those who were intent on painting this as either the judgement of God or the control of the government.

Families began to fracture over things as small as masking. Neighbors and friends began to spar concerning vaccination and political affiliations. Theories of prevention and treatment permeated the internet and in social circles. The political leadership of the United States was divided on whether it was a political distraction or a viable threat. And death began to cover the land with no discrimination of who would be next. There was no difference in the death of a poor person or a rich person, an old person or a young person or political party membership.

I began monitoring it focused on the burden of God.

The pandemic caused more than a medical and social upheaval. It caused an individual review of faith and worship practices. It made me go back to God with inquiry. This was just as much a struggle for me as when I was first saved and given religious jargon to spout and quirky gyrations to prove my salvation. I could act the part but had no part in the reality of faith, relationship, and discipleship. It almost shipwrecked my life during that era.

COVID-19 was unheard of unless one wished to follow the news and other social media postings. Many adults in my circle were aware of it yet not concerned at that time. I began monitoring it focused on the burden of God. I observed where it was an issue 'overseas' before it began coming to the shores of America. I viewed it just like the HIV/AIDS issue when it was "over there" and not in America. Just with logical thought I assumed with the technology of travel and just human nature that it would spread, and fast! Yet, many had no thoughts of this affecting their everyday lives and rituals, especially church functions.

Fear-based theology cannot work unless you have captives in your congregation.

In that era everything was intact and predictable. Then the lockdowns began. This "thing" that everyone knew would not get to them was now on the verge of disrupting everything known to us concerning faith, comfort, and life. From the time of introduction to the world until the time of personal affect, COVID was not something to be taken lightly.

We were returning to the reality that the Church was built on prayer and the Word of God, not choirs, praise and worship songs and programs.

Fear-based theology cannot work unless you have captives in your congregation. But if you cannot hold the congregation captive and guilt trip someone into giving under these circumstances then your only relief would be that sound and proper doctrine was taught and operated in prior to the pandemic. We as the Body of Christ began a warp-speed transition from faith to faith and glory to glory with the stakes of everlasting life exceedingly high. We were returning to the reality that the Church was built on prayer and the Word of God, not choirs, praise and worship songs and programs. All of us were being evaluated concerning our faith. And we could no longer retreat to our spiritual enclaves locking the doors behind us in existential cowardice.

It was hard to see how Romans 8:28 was at work in this unless one is reserved to the truth (not fact since they change) that God is in control of everything. I kept reminding myself of a time when I (foolishly) questioned God concerning something that was "prima facia" concerning His actions! I can describe the smooth rebuke that I remember to this day.

I was in quite a bit of pain from injuries and other things with military service. I had endured surgery that was so painful until there were times when I did not want to see or hear anyone or anything including my beloved dog who stayed at my side through it all. I began asking God how this pain was working together for my good. He gently and smoothly reminded me of the full passage and its meaning. He gave me four words which took hold in my spirit. "According to His purpose" became my mantra. All this time I was focused on the "good" not the "His." Well, this nugget is what really has encouraged and kept me during that season.

I can say with all humility that I was NOT the strong and unmovable man that I thought I was approaching.

In this work, I pray someone will be blessed by a candid and transparent recollection of thoughts and concerns during a time when nothing was left unturned. I can say with all humility that I was NOT the strong and unmovable man that I thought I was approaching. Instead, I was that "guy" who was INCREASINGLY calling on God for everything. The new revelation of Proverbs 3:5,6 gave me the freedom and liberty to walk through life continuously asking His guidance, sometimes even audibly in public! While I do not make this a habit there have been instances where I asked aloud with strangers present, "Now what Lord"? I mean, after all society has endorsed stranger practices. Yet, with this era on earth many more are practicing the same.

A couple of friends of mine who help with a myriad of things in society have ascribed a saying to me. They say to call Ernest and ask him to "put a little Jesus on it." It is their way of asking me to pray for a situation or direction we were going in concerning our objective. I certainly obliged the request. And the outcome has always been favorable (although sometimes delayed as favorable) outcome. But I learned that principle because of the COVID-19 pandemic. So, while others may not agree, this is another abstract proof of Romans 8:28!

Ask before not after your malady of error in actions.

While I don't ascribe to luck or karma, I do practice the principles of sowing and reaping. I prefer to receive a harvest instead of tit for tat. To my knowledge there is no word for coincidence in Biblical Hebrew. Why would there be when we are the children of an omniscient, omnipresent, and omnipotent God? Yet we often feel the unnecessary need to help God run the universe since He should have contacted us for information on creating it. This is where I discovered that I need to inquire about Him before I make any decision, not after! There is no need to lock the barn door after the horse is stolen. It is too late then. The same principle applies to walking with God. Ask before not after your malady of error in actions.

In my "putting a little Jesus on it" for whatever choice we were facing, I was asking nothing but what God wanted me to do. Pastor Jerome Lewis of Seeds of Greatness Bible Church was immeasurable in this season for many lives, especially mine. One of his quotations that stuck with me during a sermon on asking God for direction was, *"Wisdom is knowing what to do when you don't know what to do."* I quoted that to someone, and they looked at me like a cow glaring at a new gate. Yet I understand it fully. I can only know what to do when I do not know what to do unless God tells me! Oh well. Some will. Some will not. So what? (An old Amway adage).

THE BEGINNING

Late in 2019 reports began surfacing about a SARS virus that had emerged in China. Initially, there was no concern. Many thought that it would be contained in China like many other illnesses or that a method of prevention would stop it from entering the United States. This was furthest from the truth. I am convinced that there was an outbreak in the United States before we as a population were alerted.

During the Thanksgiving holiday of 2019 my wife and I enjoyed dinner at a swank hotel on the East Coast. It was a lovely dinner in an exquisite location. All would have been wonderful except for the "atmosphere." While dining I noticed that more than a few people were gagging and coughing; some like they could not breathe. I made up my mind to hurriedly finish this gourmet meal and make haste to the valet while covering my face with a handkerchief. Well, my wife would not have me walking through this hotel looking like I was a bourgeois bandit. But you know how I feel in this scenario.

We departed for our drive home and discussed it the whole way. It was amazing how our expectations were shattered with quickness due to the hacking and sniffling of the venue. I thought we walked into a live petri dish with human size germs! About two days later we were both sick and in bed. I was worse. I felt like I was beaten with a bag of nickels and nails. I have contracted the flu before and none of the instances were like this feeling. I had never felt anything like it. I could hardly breathe or stay up. I kept praying and speaking the Word. After a couple of weeks, we were both better and moving around. This is when it started to hit the nation.

I often grieve with no outward signs or duress, just emotionless.

Early in 2020 I was required to travel to various locations in the country. My first trip was to Arkansas for a gathering and reunion concerning an assignment in the military. It had been organized and planned well in advance. In fact, most of it was planned on the foundation of an earlier festival and remembrance ceremony. I was heavy with grief while in transit. An incredibly special person in my life in both ministry and personal life was terminally ill. He had taken a turn for the worse and was hospitalized. I was grieving harder than I showed others. I often grieve with no outward signs or duress, just emotionless. During that time, I realized that I suffered from a condition that is brought on by stress, pain, injury, or a rise in calcium in the bloodstream, all related to my military service and assigned to clean up nuclear material. Well, the stress of the impending loss was too much along with the physical pain of traveling.

My body informed me of the need for immediate treatment.

While my hotel was directly across the street from an urgent care center it did not open for another few hours. I did what any strong warrior would do. I googled the nearest emergency room. That is where I headed at 4 am for treatment of this excruciating pain that had begun wracking my body. I was affected by an episode of pseudo gout which attacks joints with inflammation and pain with crystals and bounces to other areas. It is caused by fluctuating levels of calcium in the blood and thyroid abnormalities caused by radiation cleanup in the military.

I was treated very quickly luckily. While standing at the window to finish my discharge instructions I received the call that he had passed away. While I knew this moment would be upon me soon, I still was hit with the blow of loss while in pain in a foreign location. This was the beginning of hearing the initial blows of COVID as well.

As I was leaving the hospital campus, I overheard a couple speaking of people that could not breathe and were being taken to the area hospitals. I thought nothing of it at the time. I only wanted to connect with the people that I had come to connect with and begin my grieving process for someone that would surely be missed by many. Yet this was the beginning of my sorrows for the COVID pandemic. While this friend had not died because of COVID, his passing began a host of challenges due to the pandemic and gathering in such an environment.

I was returning from Arkansas when I overheard airport employees speaking of shutting down all flights in the future days. I did not think it was that serious to do such a thing. Yet, I pondered what would come of such a move if it were to occur. Eventually it did. I am so glad that I did not have to deal with flight cancellations, rescheduling or the basic pandemonium that ensued.

Upon return it would be another two weeks for the memorial to be arranged. Due to familial and geographical challenges there had to be more than one celebration of his life. I chose to drive to Georgia instead of flying because of the concern in scheduling or the cancellations that were looming. By this time momentum for a shutdown was increasing. The drive was long but necessary. When I arrived, I could sense concern and fear in the community in Northern Georgia. Some people were clearly living in fear. Other people were borderline arrogant (ignorant) and cocky concerning the virus. We were careful and quickly departed once we spoke truth to the situation of religious arrogance caused by ignorance and the pandemic.

My emotions were a mix of confusion, anger, and frustration at the observations of "church folk" who had no inkling of the danger yet thought they could "praise dance" their way through this. While I know God is able, He also tells us to ask for wisdom. But, with all the confusion and flippant declarations there were bound to be casualties just from religious malpractice and religious presumption.

As quoted in "The Community of We," "The culture of fear profits from the culture of fear."

As we continued driving home, I was constantly in prayer. I had begun thinking of the damage many would suffer because of misinformation, misplaced faith, and plain ignorance of the pandemic's possibilities. In my lifetime I do not recall any pandemic of this nature and devastation. I do recall the HIV/AIDS virus beginning to spread. But I did not recall anything of this nature. As with anything that causes fear, the media will surely put their spin on it. As quoted in "The Community of We," *"The culture of fear profits from the culture of fear."* During the AIDS epidemic fear was cast on certain populations and practiced behaviors. Such fear continues to perpetuate suspicion and can even grow violent through ignorance. Now, we were in such a frenzy concerning this virus that it had many origins but no ending in sight.

In my lifetime I do not recall any pandemic of this nature and devastation.

Political jousting caused many to suffer while misinformation and distrust was sown. Many watched as society redefined who was essential personnel and who was expendable. I was confused at how some were considered essential personnel and others were not. Even the businesses were being directed in ludicrous manners.

I read the list of businesses that were allowed to be open as essential. I was totally floored to discover that liquor stores were considered essential operations. Their status was impacting since many would add an additional burden to medical treatment facilities if people were to go into withdrawal with delirium tremens (DTs). It made sense to me once I began giving it logical thought.

I was totally floored to discover that liquor stores were considered essential operations.

I witnessed (and heard over the phone) fear from every angle. I began to continually declare Psalms 91 over family, home, friends, and anyone that came to my mind. Many contingency plans were not sufficient to handle the pandemic because nothing of this nature had happened prior to it. Grocers were inundated with shoppers who were hoarding everything from toilet paper to meat and of course hand sanitizer.

I was on a military base shopping at a commissary when I observed the pandemonium. First there were limits on those allowed on the military base. Then there was the line at the door of the commissary and the various "priority" groups allowed to shop at various hours. Once inside I witnessed veterans and others on active duty almost come to blows over packs of meat. I never expected to witness this, especially on a secure military base.

I began to continually declare Psalms 91 over family, home, friends, and anyone that came to my mind.

The redeeming quality was watching those who were not ready to result in fisticuffs. I watched who would gather dried beans, rice, smoked meat, and other staples that would sustain a family. *I was one of them.* I knew I could be sustained with my superior culinary abilities to produce what I call "cowboy or hobo" meals. I gathered about ten pounds of beans with ten pounds of rice in my cart. Then while everyone decided to "throw hands" over the fresh meat I was collecting the smoked meat that was abandoned in the freezer. I wish I could have secured some salted herring that was a staple for us growing up for breakfast.

As I was leaving and heading to the cashier (they were still battling at the meat counter) I secured two gallons of oil and three bags of flour with butter and jelly. Combined with the contents of my freezer and household we were amazingly comfortable. Yet, I still could not decipher the unnatural need to hoard toilet paper. Some things will be answered in the by and by.

I knew I could be sustained with my superior culinary abilities to produce what I call "cowboy or hobo" meals.

For the next several weeks what was considered the normal day turned into a form of confinement. Initially, I was content with being at home with my family and friends. Then reports began to emerge of those who contracted the virus, who were hospitalized and who passed away due to complications. I was under a heavy blur with so many deaths and hospitalizations. Healthcare professionals who were adamant about COVID not being deadly or even a true virus began infections and sometimes hospitalizations. I knew my best plan of action would be to stay quiet, obey the directives of the government and be safe at all costs. While it was difficult at first concerning safety measures, we could always improvise for various needs such as hand sanitizer and other antiviral actions.

This was the beginning of sorrows.

It was at this point that my faith began being tested and stretched. Even though I knew what the Bible spoke of concerning these times, it took total concentration to not be taken in by the hype of society and media broadcasts. I knew the signs of the times. I knew I had recorded things revealed in seasons of prayer and fasting. I knew this was not going to be a six-month inconvenient situation and then a miraculous return to normal. This was the beginning of sorrows. Yet, little did I know how God would use this situation to groom and grow me! All the time I was looking at things I deemed negative. Romans 8:28 and Jeremiah 29:11 is still truth. Yet, our revelation of them SHOULD have been changed and expanded. Romans 8:28 is quoted by every Christian that has been saved for a collective five minutes. We have reduced such a powerful passage to a cliché whereby we ignore a key phrase; "according to HIS will." That is where we attempt to interject OUR will.

> ***Romans 8:28 is quoted by every Christian that has been saved for a collective five minutes.***

In addition, Jeremiah 29:11 is recorded after seventy years of captivity! So how much patience were you praying to God for? It sounds ultra-holy to declare that you are waiting patiently on God. However, In the waiting, how much weight are you carrying? I hate to see what some people are looking like now as I pen this! I am sure I will not be getting any Christmas greetings for bursting some religious bubbles.

HABITUAL RITUAL

In the pandemic's early days many were displaced due to what I have coined as "habitual ritual." This phenomenon occurs when there is a practiced religious ritual that becomes a habit of necessity more than a holy activity or Christian discipline. This is what happened to those who named the name of Christ yet only used worship, prayer, and study as a checklist. Most if not all Christians have a form of a "habitual ritual" in their lives that was tested during the pandemic.

Personally, I was in the "military" mindset of which days required me to do what. Certainly, I have my daily studies and meditation. Then there was the evening prayer meeting and whether I could complete the commute or not. I could tune in through the internet, but it did not give me my Holy Ghost wrapping. It was wonderful in a sense because of the convenience. There was Bible study night and of course Sunday worship experience. I had it all mapped out on my calendar and in my mind. As with many saints, the complete week surrounds Sunday and whatever designated other days are designated. Yet, there were no boundaries concerning outside activities encroaching on those "habitual rituals" that we had established. And these rituals included meals as well.

The pandemic was an immediate wound to the population of faith.

The first instance of presumptuous faith and knee jerk reaction was in the month of March 2020 while I was at a memorial for a close friend, mentee, and brother. He was a pastor of a growing congregation. Upon his transition, there was to be temporary leadership. I witnessed the rallying cry of "we will not close our church doors because God will protect us." While this was a partial truth, God also said not to tempt Him. The pandemic was an immediate wound to the population of faith. Many were totally stressed out because they could not imagine NOT going to church as ritual because God would punish them in their minds. In the Pentecostal church that developed me you had better be in church every time the doors open AND have an offering for every basket that crossed your path at times being a steady parade of offering ushers. They were scared to miss the Rapture. So that mindset was truly upset by the pandemic.

I remember standing up and telling the congregation of my transitioned friend and young pastor that we needed to heed the directions of the government until something was planned and implemented. I did receive some looks from a few of the congregants. I did not care. And that was not the only congregation that I addressed in such a manner. I noticed that many pastors began to spew their political and social views concerning this situation, often depending on knowledge from poisoned sources. This was not limited to just one culture, but humanity-wide observations were being made.

> ***Friends were dying because of what was "labeled" as strong faith.***

Friends were dying because of what was "labeled" as strong faith. Another division was being planted; the faith-filled and the no faith people. Sadly, the "no-faith" category did not have as many casualties from my local observation. We all belong to God. While many deaths really weighed heavily on me, there were a few that were devastating because they could have been avoided. Yet, I stand firmly on God's word in Romans 14. I will not judge another man's servant regardless of agreement with them or not.

THE IMMEDIATE IMPACT

I recall hearing of a pandemic that was centered in China. I watched intently because common sense would inform us of the ability to spread beyond the borders of China. While this was used as political fodder as most things in the era, I was not ignorant of the fact that life in America as we knew it would change very rapidly. In fact, I tried to ask the Lord for which I should be preparing. It was evident that we would be amid something new and deadly.

The beginning of the COVID restrictions began as I was in Arkansas for a reunion and celebration of sorts. While there was no alarm at that time, there was discussion of the "what if" factor. I had a painful health attack that landed me in the area emergency room during the wee hours of the morning. It was so early and between "shifts" of sorts that my examination and treatment took less than ninety minutes total. As I was being discharged from medical treatment, I received a call from my godson that his father, a person close to me in life and ministry, had just passed away. It was not unexpected, but devastating, nonetheless. In retrospect the emotional, psychological, and social burden that I was carrying that day contributed to my malady, causing a visit to the emergency room. Our bodies do not respond well to stress.

> ***It was evident that we would be amid something new and deadly.***

I finished the assignment and returned home before leaving again to attend memorial services for my son in the ministry (I am not a collector of spiritual children. Just as in the natural "normal" people do not parent more than they can care for, the same is true for spiritual children). As we drove (I was not getting inside of a plane with no protection, not knowing the fullness of devastation of COVID-19) many hours to Georgia. Once the memorial service ended and the ministry had to function, I witnessed "my" first instance of religious buffoonery when told of the early deadly effect of the virus.

Many Christians were defying the direction of the government because they viewed it as an attack on God. They were calling on God to protect them without asking God if they should be doing what they were doing, period! Oh, it was a very valiant and zealous thing to say that they were NOT going to honor the government and rebel. I firmly informed them of what the Bible clearly stated about authority and did not bite my tongue concerning the ignorance of those giving the directive and those following such nonsense and trying to put God's stamp of approval on their religious buffoonery.

Such a mindset had me witness many deaths even until this day that was facilitated by those playing Russian Roulette with the pandemic. Sadly, many chose to listen to others in media or political circles and caused the deaths of some remarkably close to them if not their own deaths. A gentleman in this area was adamant about political buffoonery and his "view" on this demonic vaccine. He refused to get it, which was his respected choice. But he would not allow his spouse to receive it. He contracted the virus and brought it home. She died from it. He survived. But the guilt was overwhelmingly present each time we crossed paths. It was a silent yet solemn glance that we shared.

Many Christians were defying the direction of the government because they viewed it as an attack on God.

We were in Georgia to attend the celebration of life of an impactful pastor. I was heavy because we shared so many times of intimacy and transparency together. Yet, his final times were so heavy upon me partly because religious expectations instead of godly wisdom partially hastened his demise. That will be saved for another presentation.

On the long drive back, we were careful about where we stopped, what we did and how much we would allow ourselves to be exposed to others. Mind you, we were exposed during the prior Thanksgiving season while enjoying a holiday meal at an upscale hotel. Yet, we exercised wisdom in our contacts with others. With the immediate onset of societal quarantine, we were prepared to dig in.

I recall once we returned (this was in the early days of March 2020) EVERYTHING shut down. It was like a ghost city with nothing moving. Yes, there were stores open, but panic caused them to be ravaged. To this very day, I do not understand why in the event of an emergency the first thing people hoard toilet paper is instead of dried beans, rice, and things to sustain the need for toilet paper. I will rest at that thought. I witnessed hostilities and such evil just in line to shop at a military commissary. For a minute, there were some physical escalations at the meat coolers.

While they were there shouting and shoving, I was in the dried bean and rice aisle ensuring we had enough to sustain ourselves in the event the meat would become scarce. And meat did become a scarce commodity very quickly. Yet, growing up in a financially challenged household prepared me for times like these. When the people stopped fighting over the fresh meat, I politely and smoothly moved behind them collecting the smoked meat that was left behind.

God never said He would give us manna again.

In addition, I began honing my skills of fishing and crabbing. God never said He would give us manna again. But He did promise that we would have all our needs (food included) provided by His riches in glory. Well, his riches also included plenty of perch, catfish (I do not eat them but did give them to neighbors), an endless supply of Maryland Blue Crabs along with venison. Those in this area are also fond of other wild games which I think I can pass on at this time. I do not think I can prepare a gourmet meal utilizing squirrel (tree chicken), muskrat, beaver, groundhog or racoon. While the Lord had prepared me for such a time as this, I was tasked to show others that there was no shortage, just a restructuring of our necessities.

The impact was powerful in that it caused an alarm for things that did not need an alarm and caused callousness with the prevention of the spread of fear. Again, political wrangling is responsible for many deaths during this era. Even Christians sadly used this hideous situation to attempt furthering toxic doctrine and Christian nationalism under the guise of faith during the pandemic. I was sick to my stomach at people whose nonsense caused others to be filled with grief.

I did not argue with anyone about their convictions.

Another man in my area was adamant about his ignorant to idiotic thoughts concerning the present pandemic. He was very outwardly vocal about his "president" said this was a hoax and therefore it was a lie produced by some deep state government. He continued with his public rants. Then I did not see him for quite some time. When I saw him again in the community, he looked horrible. I discovered that with his flippant attitude and actions; he was the source of infection for his wife who died from complications of the virus as stated earlier. The guilt of his ignorant actions led to horrible consequences. I did not argue with anyone about their convictions.

Upon our quarantine I learned quite a bit about myself.

Christians especially were quick to use the Bible to justify their own actions; often using Scripture completely out of context. There was never a time when I did not express total disdain for such religious error because there was surely an immature believer that would embrace such a belief and the ensuing damage.

We had become so connected until the delivery drivers often asked what I was cooking!

Upon our quarantine I learned quite a bit about myself. A friend of mine used to tell me that my parrot wanted options. He was okay to be in his cage. But he wanted the option to come out and would really clown if you locked his cage! I now knew how he felt. I wanted that "option" of going to Walmart or even the corner gas station. Instead, I was witnessing the boom of e- commerce. United Parcel Service, United States Postal Service, Federal Express and Amazon were making ruts in my street from the constant deliveries. We had become so connected until the delivery drivers often asked what I was cooking! I had no problem feeding them either. In fact, I try to continuously provide victuals to those I am associated with so they can continue to make an impact in society without hunger pains.

We, as a society discovered that "those people" many look down upon were the very ones keeping a sense of normalcy in society.

I watched businesses that would dare to adjust to the current situation begin to flourish. Then, I watched those who refused to budge go out of business quickly because of their rigidity. Those who were employed and considered "essential personnel" ranged in identity to convenience store workers, liquor store workers and the gamut of health and safety employees. We, as a society discovered that "those people" many look down upon were the very ones keeping a sense of normalcy in society.

Health care workers were on the front lines with many beginning to show signs of Post Traumatic Stress Syndrome/Disorder. I witnessed doctors, nurses, and other technicians cry from being overwhelmed at the deaths. The health care workers that I know were working multiple shifts. And, if they were employed by skilled care facilities the virus would move quickly through those facilities attacking the most vulnerable of patients.

We also had a family member in a nursing facility during this time. I can recall having to fly to a destination the next morning. The facility had not yet been shut down to the public. The drive to the facility was approximately forty-five minutes. I called in the morning right as everyone was arriving at work. In fact, I was on the road to ensure I could make it there in time to see him just in case they were quarantined. I was medically cleared to visit. Yet, by the time I arrived (under thirty minutes later) they had quarantined the whole facility! I did not know what to expect, so I drove home to finish packing. I can say that the facility was one of the only ones in a two to three state radius that stayed virus free for well over six months. But, when the virus did find its way in the facility, it was through the staff. The residents were not affected as much as other facilities. But there was still an effect on the population.

When you are locked in a close quarter situation with anyone, you will surely find your tender spots in your relationships.

But the most impactful effect of the pandemic was on individual households. When you are locked in a close quarter situation with anyone, you will surely find your tender spots in your relationships. I was no different. While I could find something to do, my wife was trying to help her office adjust to the present situation. I was not surprised at the governmental agencies on all levels that were not prepared for immediate distance employment.

While the technology was present, no one thought to prepare just in case there was a requirement for remote workers to function at home.

Most churches had no contingency plan in place should the need arise to fellowship and worship from a distance.

This same situation affected churches as well. Most churches had no contingency plan in place should the need arise to fellowship and worship from a distance. Most churches had programs in place to better accommodate those people who chose to come in person. The in-person attendance also allowed various techniques and practices to continue thereby continuing tradition even in giving. But, once the physical presence was removed, there was a problem with the techniques that had been past practice.

I listened to pastors and their leaders twist conspiracy theories about online giving or any other type of electronic and distance contributions. I heard so many "theories" until I could not entertain any conversations about giving especially if they were bullied or coerced to give. Since God loves the cheerful giver, then He will not twist your arm. That is simple to me. Yet, there were churches and clergy speaking doom and gloom if you did not give as they said.

Since God loves the cheerful giver, then He will not twist your arm.

Then there were churches whose focus was never on money but prosperity. I say prosperity apart from money because money is the lowest form of prosperity. Those fellowships that became beacons of hope and assistance to the community grew in every area including membership. One church in my region became such a beacon until their financial contributions almost doubled along with becoming a point of relief for the region. All of this was accomplished without anything but past prolific preaching and teaching and the desire to help everyone. All did not decline in this area. Many churches excelled.

THE FAITH DISCREPANCIES

It can be totally disturbing when something happens and the first thing that a religious person will attack you with (in the middle of something already attacking) is the accusation or idiotic assumption that you do not have enough faith. This happened almost immediately when the pandemic unleashed its potential in the early days. I was hurt by the number of clergy people telling, almost commanding their assigned congregants to NOT obey the government or take proper precautions and try to tie the desire to do so to a lack of faith. Romans 14 gave me much understanding in my personal role of faith. My faith is my faith. And, the Bible says we were given "the" measure of faith which told me that my faith has the potential to be unlimited.

Yet, there can be fake faith. So many cliches have been thrown out for eons on faith until many have no idea of scriptural reference of faith. But those same individuals can tell you every cliché that sounds theologically sound to the novice of Bible reading. Many were sincere in their declarations.

I already had much admiration for those in the health care industry before COVID-19.

Without revealing identities, I have discovered many pastors and members died because of their choices and convictions. Do I lambast them in their demise? NO. I do grieve for the surviving families. It has and still is an extremely challenging time for the ministry in this area due to the varied and often scattered beliefs. Prominent pastors of influential congregations even left this earth because they stated that it was God's will for none to receive the vaccinations. They also were stating that all must continue to gather regardless of the governmental mandates, science recommendations and medical necessities. They did not care that the hospitals were overwhelmed, and health care workers were under horrible strain. I already had much admiration for those in the health care industry before COVID-19. But the pandemic brought out just how much those rarely seen individual including those where were considered "essential personnel" were. The workers of convenience stores and even liquor stores (I did not understand that one fully) were deemed essential to the operation of society! Can you believe it? Those "people" that work in those "jobs" were ESSENTIAL in your everyday existence.

I was a bit perplexed to know that liquor stores were considered essential operations. I railed against that logic. But, in the interest of listening to opposing opinions I discovered that if the liquor stores just shut down it would be catastrophic. As much as I did not want to believe it. That statement was true. I did not realize how many alcohol-dependent people there are in society. The hospitals were already overwhelmed with virus victims. If liquor stores closed the facilities would surely be pushed beyond limits because of extreme withdrawal from alcohol. I had no idea how interwoven alcoholism was in American society. While focus was given on other substances particularly opioids, alcohol already had a stronghold and was rooted deep among the people. Even to the point of switching their purpose for manufacturing, much of the alcohol was being made into hand sanitizer to maximize profits since no one was going out to drink.

No one cares about faith until it is tested.

With all this happening everywhere, we should not try to measure another's faith, but ensure our faith is operational and highly active. No one cares about faith until it is tested. That is a hard pill to swallow. We are taught that we grow from faith to faith. American believers became complacent in their faith since we were the "land of plenty" according to many Evangelicals in America.

Now, to address the issue of denominations, evangelicals and just plain cultish radicals, everyone had a faith declaration concerning this pandemic and all the politics surrounding it. I grew increasingly annoyed at Evangelicals and others encouraging those in the Christian faith to defy governmental recommendations and statues because it was a challenge to their "religious freedom." This is not a work to unravel some misguided beliefs. I am just identifying some of the aspects that damaged Christianity's influence because of fringe groups.

I recall a prophetic conference that had been planned for quite some time prior to the pandemic. But, when the pandemic rose, the conference was not cancelled. Instead, many were encouraged to attend and did. I must admit I genuinely wanted to attend having initially made plans. But common sense in my mind was to stay at home and hope for a streaming platform due to safeguarding my family's health who were immunocompromised. That did not happen. Like those in other locations that I implored to stay safe by allowing this gathering to pass, there were people here that felt for me even to suggest they not attending was akin to blasphemy. Yet there was one person who it was part of his destiny to face this after a powerful worship session.

Too often a prophetic word of wisdom or knowledge is given. The messenger could become tiffed if the person chose to not take "heed" to the message. I believe a brother who quietly affected many lives was such a person to have a choice to serve God in such a capacity.

Someone who opened a door for me in my youth attended a planned conference without fear. This man who touched many lives grew up in the Washington, D.C. area of Lamond Riggs. His quiet way of sorts was a beacon personally to me. I am sure he was not quiet in other things on the playground. The church that I saw him in was a short distance from his neighborhood but in the middle of mine. He told Mr. Vernon Taylor (the Scoutmaster) that he knew some boys that may want (he said needed) to be Boy Scouts. Mind you, I have no idea to this day whether he was one. But he recommended it to us. We were a group of mischievous, borderline little urchins out of control. Out of that "recommendation" came many societal blessings that were not in position, a highly professional photographer, a very high-ranking enlisted man in the Air Force, a few distinguished military personnel, helicopter mechanic and a seminarian. These are the outcomes that we know of.

He was also a quiet yet powerful worshipper. I was taken back to discover he attended, contacted COVID-19, was hospitalized, and transitioned to heaven with his family outside the window worshiping as he transitioned. I did not see any reason this had to occur other than the humanistic need to be right and in the place that society dictated. Yet that was not his reason!

In communicating with his family to ensure he is represented in the correct and truthful manner I discovered more than I thought. (I already knew him as a powerful man of God.) Not only did he commit himself to lead worship that night, but he also had no fear of it. This is why his choice to lead worship is so impactful, especially to me! This was a person that knew of possible and even probable danger yet continued because he felt in the deepest recesses of his spirit that God directed him. He experienced an Acts 21:11 sort of warning if he continued as he intended and did not shrink from the possibility of danger but made a choice. He respected the situation fully knowing the dangers. Yet he chose to do the will of God as pertaining to his life. We may never know on this side of glory what he accomplished in those moments. But just as he could not see what we would become, he was obedient in his recommendation to us. I have gleaned and continued to glean nuggets of faith from his life.

His family relayed to me while hospitalized he was still concerned about the health and well-being of others, especially the nursing staff. This brought a tear to my eye. His ongoing love and concern for others continued to be a part of his existence. His daughter stated that he wished others would have understood how severely the virus affected the human body. Even with the effects of COVID he was still concerned about the health care workers' well-being.

There is no way a person possesses that much peace without the Prince of Peace present with him.

The reason I say that he embraced this destiny is that he continually exuded peace in this complete situation. It's impossible to possess that much peace without the Prince of Peace present with him. His daughter and I both believe that he was not alone in his transition to heaven. His powerful faith and worship assure me that he is now in the presence of the King, ushered in the Kingdom by angels. This is the only example that I can think of, which was not done out of rebellion but out of love and obedience. His surviving family still honors him in memory and their continued worship and discipleship of God. This man was a victor in all definitions of the word.

The same situation was with a young aspiring pastor in the northeastern area of the United States. However, he was being rebellious and politically motivated by internet theories and platforms. He was torn between the pageantry of Episcopalian worship and the firebrand, nothing but the Authorized King James Version of 1611 (straight bibliotry) and no salvation apart from baptism. This was the beginning of his demise. Even in his staunch adherence to the KJV, his additional problem was with the desired subservience of women. I am not sure where this "doctrine" came from, but he felt that women were subservient to men. We locked horns on that topic many, many times. His wife was discharged from the hospital. He never was. Situations like this truly wounded me; knowing that a life was lost because of religious restriction with political poison.

I am sure I can go on for quite some time with many examples of distorted faith. But it would serve no purpose. The point is clearly made. Many said they were following the Lord's direction to disobey civil and spiritual authority. While some spiritual authorities were browbeating many that questioned the validity of being instructed to disobey the government, many were castigated and even excommunicated as being part of the devil's mission. Yet in all the examples that were presented to me at the beginning of this it was only ONE that rose above the rest. And his family truly allowed us to partake of the gift of God in their lives. Others tried to stand out for whatever reason.

> ***These fake remedies along with various political conspiracies contributed to unnecessary deaths.***

Again, I was taken back at how much misinformation was being strewn across social media. Cures from drinking warm water every fifteen minutes to flush the virus into the stomach acid to kill it to burning sage in your house and air ducts were being forwarded over many media outlets. These fake remedies along with various political conspiracies contributed to unnecessary deaths. I was and still am appalled at how many people will blindly follow the masses into death and destruction all in the name of faith; misguided faith at that! This is valid proof that too much information can be more dangerous than not having enough!

Yet I had to come to grips with my own struggles which I really had not understood until well into the lockdown. The pandemic removed all barriers and escape mechanisms in relationships, especially marriages. I was not required, for lack of better words, to go to a place of worship. I was taken back for a bit because of this. I had become accustomed (and familiar sadly) with going to a house of worship for a connection to others that had become ritualistic. Now, there was no ritual. I was lost. Yet, I began digging into my own spirit to find what was lacking in me.

We become complacent in knowing that on assigned dates and weekends we are "expected" to be gathered as saints in locations.

What I discovered that I was lacking was not the desire, but the understanding of why it is necessary to remain connected to God in all aspects. We become complacent in knowing that on assigned dates and weekends we are "expected" to be gathered as saints in locations. This begins the ritual that will sidetrack all believers into a "law and work" mentality instead of a "grace and flow" function. Those that could punch their respective righteous reports to having attended church that week were now at a deficit for their "works." We all felt that happen.

I did witness many innovative measures to worship, though. I discovered my nephew would wake up his family, ensure everyone got dressed, and they would go downstairs and worship in the media or online. This preserved the ritualistic travel outside of comfort and complacency. Ironically, I used to give many of these same examples when you work from home. Get up, go out one door, come in another and get to work. One would be surprised at the boost that gives your psyche.

In my own home we would sit on the couch taking notes and checking references the same as we would be in the sanctuary. Those fellowships that began moving with the cloud prior to the pandemic were able to absorb much of the social shock. I say social shock because many had not learned to discipline and art of worship, but only church.

> *In my own home we would sit on the couch taking notes and checking references the same as we would be in the sanctuary.*

Dr. Hart Ramsey once stated, "We are highly developed in church." He expounded on that truth that we know how to do things related to church service, but do not understand why. He truly released a truth to those who could catch it. Another dearly departed friend of mine would state that many congregations were so busy "churching" until they would not allow the Holy Spirit to move. I agreed with him on one point. The point that we differed on was that many never knew if He was moving or whether learned behavior in the guise of a dance was the motivation. The 'holy dance' is often the measurement in many fellowships of the Holy Spirit's movement among the people. Sadly, this activity is often accompanied by shouts of "praise Him while you can" or "you better praise Him." Again, man needed understanding in the form of ritual and scheduled activity.

I was looking in the mirror and did not like what I discovered about myself. I had passively fallen into the ritualistic worship of my Lord.

Please do not think I was not affected by all of this. I was just as affected as anyone else with one exception. I was looking in the mirror and did not like what I discovered about myself. I had passively fallen into the ritualistic worship of my Lord.

HORRORS! Without realizing it, I had begun worshiping in a very ritualistic manner.

We as saints must always keep our praise and worship fresh.

Yes, I was on fire for praise and worship. Yet, I was not on fire for recognizing those things needing attention such as a focused study on worship. We as saints must always keep our praise and worship fresh. This is more than just being pumped up with music. We must have those moments of quiet and meaningful worship that overwhelm and do not have to be inside the walls of an edifice.

I was taken up and away so powerfully until I pulled over at a rest stop, got out of the car and continued worshipping!

I can recall worship while driving listening to a song by Mercy Me; I Can Only Imagine. I was taken up and away so powerfully until I pulled over at a rest stop, got out of the car and continued worshipping! People were driving by and looking at me. But I did not care what anyone thought at that moment. It is moments like these that we forfeit because of a need for ritual and routine. Mr. COVID 19 just wrecked our comfort and routine. And I am glad for me.

In truthful observation we have a routine in Christianity.

A very stunning discovery in my own life was that I did not realize that my faith was tied to work in many unmonitored ways. In truthful observation we have a routine in Christianity. Often, we awake in the morning giving a rote prayer to the atmosphere (truly not to our loving God) followed by a reading of Scripture and then we progress to praying over food to complete the foundational rituals of Christianity. I found myself having slipped into this abyss as well. It is something like this that was brought on by the pandemic that made me take a hard look at what I was doing and why. Thank God we were with a "positioned" fellowship that had no idea of what was coming. Yet, the Pastor heeded prophetic words and continued doing what was told. I can only say that God does nothing without telling His prophets first. We must listen to Him and them.

This period of adjustment and introspection was turbulent to say the least. First, the initial alarms of your own individual inadequacy are deafening. There is no way that any human on this earth can say they cannot see anything wrong with their existence. If that were stated, I am sure it would be the most prolific lie in the universe. I would even say it would be akin to a massive multiplication of self-deception.

Next the truth and proof coming from those in your household whether spouse or mouse confirms our flaws. I was not floored but taken back at the number of divorces during the pandemic. While I do not make light of being in close quarters with people, it can be a harrowing existence. Even in the military we had escapes of sorts to put space and distance between people. In the pandemic we were stuck. The song "Love the One You Are With" became a test of love.

But conflict always precedes peace.

In honesty I learned much about myself that needed attention. Some of what I learned personally is that I can operate in a passive-aggressive state without thinking. I was too passive in past times that were the foundation of conflict at the present. There is nothing wrong with being passive. But conflict always precedes peace. My problem was that I wanted peace without any type of conflict. It just was not so. I discovered that not all conflicts are devastating. This is a truth that is not taught to young people. Depending on what your family structure was, you could never have learned this truth because your parents never mastered it. Mine did not. Conflict was always viewed as war not just disagreement. I am glad the military taught me different things. This era really caused many to review "how" they were raised. We had to come face to face with things we thought were normal only to discover that they were askew from the center position of societal existence. It is not normal to be in the presence of a person for 1,440 minutes, 24 hours a day, and 365 days a year. It can really strain relationships; and did contribute to the demise of many even in the Body of Christ.

PROPHETIC PSYCHOSIS

A very disturbing phenomenon became known during this pandemic. I termed it "prophetic psychosis." So many "prophets" emerged to have to answer this situation. They were prophesying concerning the cause or reason this pandemic appeared. Most stated that it was due to something not being accomplished by the populations of the world.

Oh, there were so many prophecies until I began blocking MOST religious and prophetic feeds from social media and unsubscribing to many emails that I often would receive. I never thought that there would be a time when such an activity would take place. I saw so many predictions of the Second Coming, who was God's pick for our government and a myriad of other wacky presentations.

Recently I was in a store when a person made a statement concerning the 2020 election. My mouth bounced off the floor after I heard a pastor in this region state to the person (he obviously did not know the man) that election was stolen. He continued stating that God, Himself, would vindicate those who lost and *supernaturally* reinstall the losing president back to power. I asked him if he could provide a witness to his prophecy or a Scriptural reference. He said, "Every true Christian knows this." So, my next question posed to him was inviting a definition of a 'true' Christian. He excitedly told us (a small group had gathered) that ALL "true" Christians would know that they must stand up and "reinstall" the losing politician. I must say that he really believed this so much as to say that any other believer that did not espouse this belief was a servant of the devil.

What I witnessed was Christians appealing loosely to the Supernatural to cosign their malarkey.

I am not a spring chicken at all. Yet, I have never witnessed such political and theological buffoonery mixed into a punch in my lifetime! I am not sure why this was not challenged by believers who study the Word of God in the beginning. But like all other conspiracies, there must be some inkling of possibilities. What I witnessed was Christians appealing loosely to the Supernatural to cosign their malarkey. I do not think God cares about political party. Remember He is the Theocrat, not Democrat. It was even so crazy until it was being spread out that if you were not of a certain political party, you were of the devil. It is a travesty of citizenship that one must choose a political party, anyway. This did not just start in 2020. I saw inklings of this madness during the previous two administrations.

I will emphatically state that America is not a Christian nation.

At the possibility of making the reader close this book and label me a heretic, I will emphatically state that America is not a Christian nation. It is one founded on Judeo-Christian morals. But America is not a Christian nation. Yet the intolerance over even various denominations saddens me. Christ told us that if we keep two commandments (love God with everything in our being and love our neighbors as ourselves that we have fulfilled all the law. Our problem is that we do not have love for ourselves. Therefore, we cannot freely love our neighbors. The pandemic shined a very bright light on neighborly love. It could be seen in the open stores, on the road and even in the medical facilities. There was no love that extended from us to our neighbors. Even neighbors were fighting over what one should do during this pandemic.

My faith is still intact.

I chose to stay safe and within the confines of my own residence. My faith is still intact. Yet I chose the route of least exposure. Why did I choose this? I chose it because my decision was bound to affect more people than just me. It would begin to affect my family, my community as well as those that I met. People were refusing to wear protective equipment because they felt that their rights were being violated. I had one question for them. What about the other person's rights since all our actions affect others? I will not even record in this medium the answers that I received. It sickened me. Romans 14 clearly states that we are not to be an occasion for another person stumbling! Could that stumble also be included in this situation? Definitely. And it is this thought that I embraced fully when deciding whether to be vaccinated. The vaccination was not to totally prevent the virus. It was to ensure that the attack of the virus was not as brutal if at all brutal. It made perfect sense to me.

I never could grasp mentally the concept of trying to reduce my omniscient, omnipotent, omnipresent God to a political party and much less a flawed candidate! But there were many "prophetic" utterances to justify something that God is allowing us to care for, election of viable officials.

Sadly, I have even lost friends due to their political stance. They had not even thought of the stark possibility that God could be speaking to each of us for a specific action that could be contrary to another's direction. A powerful pastor once told me that God is so unique that He could speak to two people at the exact same moment, telling them to completely different things. I agree! The Lord told Moses to go to Pharoah and tell him that He said to let His people go. Yet God spoke to Pharoah as well, hardening his heart. I can imagine the conversation going like this.

Moses: God sent me to tell you to let His people go!

Pharoah: I heard from your God, too. He said I can have a hard heart and not let you all go anywhere.

Think about it....

Yet so many prophetic voices forgot to be still and listen to know God. I do realize that we know His voice. So, when did the voice of God begin coming through media, politicians, lobbying groups, and special interest groups? I rest my case.

Prophetic psychosis is such a distraction and disruption until it is a war zone to walk into church with a party pin on your lapel! One day I wore a blue tie and was approached by a man who wanted to know if I was a Democrat. It caught me by surprise. But, with such a quick tongue as I have been blessed with, I could recover and toss him something to think about. I told him that I wore my blue tie to match my underwear and socks. He stood there befuddled while I walked away to purchase my lunch. He followed me out of the store to ask the question again. I told him that I was not registered with any political party until God formed one. He did not want to argue with that answer. I am saddened by the travesty of freedom. Do you mean that I must pick one party over another? I cannot. They are two wings on the same bird. And unless the body can use both wings effectively, there will never be progress. Yet we have prophets declaring your demise and the end of our country unless we support and assist who they are saying should be in power. I do not get it.

<u>The enemy of a prophet is pride amplified by time. And time is also a revealer of the heart's intentions.</u>

SOCIAL MEDIA HANDICAP

Immediately upon restrictions being made, social media became essential to many of the immediate populations. This was true of the Body of Christ as well. We began to look toward the media whether the internet or on cable TV. This was our outside connection with the population.

In walking the dog there was often when someone came out of the house just to pet the dog.

It was said that many pets were either purchased or adopted during this time. I can recall seeing an increase in social media posts featuring the new fur additions to the population. While I already owned two wonderful dogs, I could see the need for outside companionship regardless of the species. My boys (Standard Poodles) were with me constantly and enjoyed the constant companionship of their humans. On the other hand, those without pets living alone had an extremely demanding time mentally and emotionally. In walking the dog there were times when someone came out of the house just to pet the dog.

Yet, social media posed a marked danger. It was the floodgate of information, both bad and good. True information was being considered false. During this time, I viewed a documentary that stated that false information travels six times faster over social media than truth. This shocked me immensely. Yet, I was seeing this constantly during the pandemic. As I stated previously, cures were being posted with false proof and giving false hope. I cringe at the thought that many of the deaths could have been attributed to false health protection and information. The President of the United States at that time said to drink bleach. It was stated that he said it in jest. Yet, how many people took that as scientific authority and tried it?

In the beginning of the internet and social media craze one needed not worry about so much being disseminated. I recall times when you received a disc to install various media resources there was twenty hours a month's free access. The catch to that was after your initial free hours for the price the overages were horrendous. And it was already connected to your telephone bill.

Anything intended for good has the capacity to be used for evil.

I mistakenly went over my limit and received one of the hideous bills in my mail. It cured me from being non-attentive toward the clock. Even with the genesis of internet exposure, false and misleading information was being given to those subscribing to it as truth. Anything intended for good has the capacity to be used for evil. This technology is no different.

But much good did come through this technology. Churches that were viewed as progressive were already in position to broadcast from a distance. Others used resources of social media to begin a transition, not knowing how long this would last. And being proactive surely was better than reacting.

In retrospect concerning technology, I can recall when I overheard my aunt stating that the television was a "hell a vision." A humorous memory is of my younger brother being sent there during the summer for a visit. I came home on leave from the military unannounced, but my brother was not home. My mother told me where he was. So, I called. My aunt told me that he said our mother told him to come home and had already paid for his ticket. I knew my mother had not summoned him. So, I went to the bus depot to meet the bus he was on. I shocked him badly!

He told me he was running away from her because of her religious beliefs. He was not allowed to watch anything but religious shows and the news. He could not play with kids on the block because they were sinners. So, he came home. I had to laugh because to this day my mother never knew that he had run away from our aunt. I am sure they are all in glory now laughing about that time. And I wonder if my aunt stopped dressing like she is homely to prove her holiness.

Faith truly comes by hearing. But we must be careful of what we hear.

I diverted to a humorous memory because it is the precursor to this time. Technology during this time is so open and inviting until it can be a "hell a vision" of sorts. The internet and cable television began to bombard our minds. Whatever a person hears will impact on the way they live and think. It was proven during this period for the political and medical arenas. Faith truly comes by hearing. But we must be careful of what we hear.

Be careful and examine all that you have allowed into your ear and eye gates. During this era there were multiple distractions for your eyes and ears. While some churches were discovering technology, others were already in the flow. And even more people found they could hustle many in the name of God. Sadly, the church of our living God was a main attraction in the news especially for health and political buffoonery.

I recall a few articles reporting on things that are in no way indicative of Christianity nor are normal in churches. One instance was particularly disturbing. A clergyman was robbed during a televised service. The media had a field day reporting on it. Sadly, they had a field day digging into his past just to discredit him. And there was certainly monologue concerning the value of jewelry he was "walking around with." I questioned this.

It was about that time that I disconnected from television and most social media. I limited my news intake because of this. I noticed that Christianity was in the headlines quite a bit especially heralding political candidates and Christian nationalism. Yes, I did call it out. Why? Because even if America was founded on Judeo-Christian values, it cannot be a Christian nation and hold true the Declaration of Independence, the Constitution, or the Bill of Rights. Sadly, many performed various acts in the name of God when He had nothing to do with it. So, the social media trap served as a main distraction and weight for us concerning our Kingdom mandate.

REALITY WAS ELUSIVE

In the beginning of the restrictions, it was considered a pain to have to deal with being quarantined and having movements restricted. However, I still say it was a blessing, albeit a painful one. When we thought we had something totally under control we quickly discovered that being around people constantly played chords on our nerves. Those whom we considered 'safe' now became origins of close contact stress. This was especially true with my spouse and me.

With me enjoying outdoor activities such as fishing, crabbing and just listening to nature, I found many times that was the best posture to take: go fishing. But depending on why and how you left, there may have been the same issue awaiting your return. My dog and I became even closer, especially after his father died a day after Christmas.

The passing of Alphie, my Standard Poodle, was a stressor that really weighed heavily on me. He was a very attentive dog because I had physical ailments often with surgery for orthopedic and other issues. He could sense when I was in pain or stressed. He would come lay his head on my Bible or my lap, whichever he could access and make me smile. I had a total hip replacement during this time. He never left my side even though I could see that he was physically in pain. The moment I began walking without the walker in the house, he distanced himself. Within two days he could not stand up when I called him. I cried like a forcefully slapped baby. I knew this was the end for him. And I was with him even as he took his last breath of life.

Let me give everyone a bit of information that will help your pet. Do not let your pet take their last breath without you if possible. Alphie looked into my eyes so trusting as he was saying thank you. I am slightly choking up as I type. Your dog needs you, their friend, master, companion, den mate, Alpha leader or whomever with them as they cross their bridge to chase sky squirrels.

I grieved for quite some time after his passing. His son/puppy knew something was not right and would not leave my side. Even now with the passing of his father it has caused him to step into his own identity as well. He is a riot now that he is alone, a total joker. Someone once told me that having a standard poodle is like having Einstein and the Three Stooges in the same body. They were right! Yet with the grace of God, we purchased the father as a pup and received one of his offspring as well. These dogs were our reprieve from the nonsense around us.

The neighbors got a treat whenever I brought them out to play. The elder poodle would pretend he was chasing the ball long enough to get the puppy interested. Then he would come and sit next to me while I threw the ball to allow the puppy to wear himself out. He would just watch like he was "passing the baton" to the next generation. All these things assisted in deepening my spiritual connection during this era.

We were relegated to two poodles and each other.

This has become an integral part of our reality. We were relegated to two poodles and each other. Our reality of one another developed in many often-abrasive ways. It is one thing to live with a person. It is quite another thing to live with them in a semi-solitary existence. I can say with realistic enthusiasm that the lockdown strengthened our marriage because we had to face issues, while other marriages crumbled. We were made aware of one another's quirks and our previous escape mechanisms, particularly work. Even now we must face often selfish desires. This was a time for self-reflection. Where could I improve my interactions with my spouse? Where could I restructure my expectations and were they realistic? Were my personal expectations based on unfounded expectations? There were so many questions to be asked, answered and in many cases ignored until the opportune time.

But the time in solitude with one another was explosively beautiful; yet dangerous. Things that are so carefully hidden can no longer be hidden. The "closeness" makes everything visible and viable as well as external distractions and threats.

A SPIRITUAL DILEMNA IN SOCIAL MEDIA

Social media has been a two-edged sword in our lives, especially during the pandemic. While I did not agree with how much information was being disseminated during the period, I did enjoy access to viable information if you verified sources. Just like anything else, we must be able to verify the information that appears.

I noticed something peculiar yet sad during the pandemic. Ministers, ministries, and everything else seemed to fill the void of people not going to church. On one hand it was a blessing for some congregations to gather remotely through various media. Some congregations had plans and operations in place prior to the lightning onset of the pandemic. Others who preached against technology in favor of old traditions were blindsided.

Then there were the congregants that could not wait for this event to have a reason to leave the churches for whatever disagreements or discrepancies they conjured up. Either way, the Body of Christ was shaken up in our traditional seats concerning true evangelism and not just church services.

I recall a couple that were staunch Christians to the point that anything against what they were taught would be considered wrong. Yet, during the pandemic I watched them grow and change mindsets. It involved issues of hospital transportation and neighbors in a same-sex marriage. Eventually the ones that were "outside" of the church became nothing but a blessing to those within the church. I observed those who were condescending under the warped guise of righteousness but were usually the ones with the greatest need! Yet they felt that God would honor their dishonor of their neighbor. I do not think that is biblical in any sense regardless of any perceived or real sin in their lives. The disciples of Christ were caught in a dilemma as to whether truthfully accept that they were in fact not living up to the Great Commission and there had to be change.

Persecution is not having to fan because the air conditioner is broken.

Even at this point after the initial shock of the pandemic there are still those holdouts that wish to blame the pandemic on everyone unholy; except themselves. There are those who wish to blame the pandemic on some conspiracy theory in which everyone and everything is the devil persecuting them. I surely say that persecution is the furthest from their understanding. Persecution is not having to fan because the air conditioner is broken. Persecution is not when your neighbor asks you to lower the volume of your praise music so they can sleep before third shift. And persecution is NOT your manager having to write you up because you refuse to follow instruction concerning safety and your Bible in the windshield of the forklift!

We can be so dramatic when I have met persecution in a person's life. There was a Chinese visitor who was appearing at a church where I was invited. I normally go to such invitations because their testimony is warning us of what IS coming to America if we are sleepy. This gentleman was an apostle; a true one. He began telling us how they would establish underground churches. They had to be a clandestine operation because of the cost of being discovered. He said that if you were caught with the Bible in his areas and provinces, you would have a year in prison or confinement for each page you had in your possession. Ironically, he also said that only portions of the Bible were available. Immediately my mind thought of the Book of Isaiah. That is no doubt a life sentence if caught with the full book! I was curious but not disrespectful. I really wanted to ask him how long he spent in jail. But I felt that would be the ultimate disrespect fueled by carnal curiosity.

I watched his motions and mannerisms. He had truly been persecuted. His body was very frail. He was younger than me yet looked much older than me. He walked with a limited and wounded gait, and he had difficulty rising from the seated position. Yet, here was this man bringing us warnings as well as exhortation. Yet this was not reported and made to go viral in social media. But Christian nationalism was the thread flying everywhere in cyberspace.

This is one of the main dilemmas we had during this time; misuse and abuse of the cyberworld. I recall during the pandemic viewing a documentary on how the internet controls much of our lives. One thought that remained from it was the fact that false information travels six times faster than truth on social media. This is not limited to "secular" irregularities. I am genuinely concerned because much of the Body of Christ believes an inordinate amount of information without being a "Berean." And now we must reel all the things and ensure what we release again is in line with the Word and will of the Lord. I have begun a double and triple check of the period. Selah.

POLARIZATION OF BEHAVIOR

There has been much done to silently destroy the Body of Christ through division. This did not begin with the COVID-19 pandemic. It has been in operation since the Upper Room. Once the disciples left the Upper Room and stepped back into society, immediately they were accused of being drunk. Yet everyone heard their language. Division.

I do not stop there. Doctrine that was loose and selectively enforced plagued the New Testament believers. Paul dealt with an issue in Corinth where a man was committing sin that even the heathen could not name. Now that is sad! As we continue through the recorded New Testament and early church history, we see all that is causing division.

When Solomon had Ecclesiastes penned, he said there is NO new thing under the sun. Why would this era be different? In his era everything that we are experiencing now he experienced which included abortion. We did not create abortions. It has been around for a while.

Too often as I research, I get pulled down a "rabbit hole" of sorts that catches my eye. One such hole took me to the walls surrounding Jericho. I do not remember the distractive source, but it was an academic archaeology source. In this source I discovered that in the walls of Jericho the bodies of aborted, stillborn, and sacrificed newborns were buried in vases. Immediately my mouth hit the desk! In my mind, God was calling them forth for a "mission" once He gave the deployment order and the wall had to be reduced to rubble. I will not delve much into this and my own thoughts. I record this to say that one cannot have all knowledge because we are in the image of God, not fully God except in Jesus Christ. That one fact gave me a slight understanding why God gave instructions like He did, not that it matters but it is impressive to know the articulate details that God views in His purpose!

I simply support the right for a person to choose which is free will.

Bring this to today's abortion issue. I really caught grief from many religious people concerning a statement I made. I stated after much prayer that I am in support of abortion "rights" according to the law which is "pro-choice." All eyes were on me. Many just joined the cause that I supported abortion which is far from the truth. I simply support the right for a person to choose which is free will. We all have free will otherwise we would be forced to do the will of God and accept salvation. Now surely, I do NOT support abortion. Yet, the individual has a choice just as all who name the name of Christ have a "choice."

The next divisive principle that I have drawn attention to is the "pro-life" stance. Pro-life does not mean only anti-abortion. Pro-life covers a myriad of examples. Assisted suicide, death penalty, end of life suicide, police brutality and a myriad of other issues are all included in the pro-life stance. Yet many do not view a complete issue. They only make new ones. This is true in many aspects of Christianity.

Bishop Gilbert Coleman of Freedom Christian Bible Fellowship once stated, "You only obey the part of the Bible that you believe." That went through me like a lightning bolt. I had listened among "saints" saying what they believe, and the rest was in "error." That is the most idiotic thing I can fathom. Either the Bible is the word of God, or it is not! However, if one took long enough to first SIT under anointed TEACHING, much would be revealed concerning those "parts" one thinks is in error. Sadly, most of it is of a financial and materialistic nature that causes the most vicious doctrine wars.

During the period preceding and even during the pandemic a Christian Nationalist Movement began heavily. Certain buzz words and promises caused most of the "Evangelical" population in America to embrace politics instead of God. It is still affecting Christianity today. The Body of Christ is divided among Americans. Some falsely claiming that America was founded as a Christian nation. I beg to differ. It was founded on some Judeo-Christian beliefs, but not all Christian beliefs. Some take this to a stretch as to the interpretation of the founding fathers as if they knew then what would be like now. I say it was begun on flawed theology if that is the case seeing that all people were NOT created equal in their understanding.

Scripture tells us that all men AND women are created equal. While many often go to various races and cultures to bemoan inequity I will just go to the white women of that era. They were not equal as the white men and property owners. Add in the injustices toward various religious groups, social cultures, races of people and there you have it. Division again. I honestly believe if we were on one accord praying for our leaders as commanded in 1 Timothy 2:1-4 power would be on display. No, I will not list it here. I really hope that you go and look it up for yourself. Be a Berean! And I pray that you will find those same rabbit holes that I often find to engage you much further than the immediate point.

There are so many issues that divide us as Christians until they are not able to be numbered. Things as simple as a Bible version or the color of a sanctuary causes division. Yet many of the things that divided us physically were no longer issues during the pandemic. But sadly, Google became the seminary for many. Not to be braggadocious but I have had to cause a few zealous wannabe theologians to back up. There are some that just will not allow you to acquiesce to them! They must either argue with you with circular reasoning or implode!

When I was at home, I discovered without accountability to someone I was surely lacking.

I am not without blame!!! During this time, I was not as diligent as I had been. And I will delve into transparency as we go on. It is much easier to continue what we consider discipline with companies who share our desire and beliefs. When I was at home, I discovered without accountability to someone I was surely lacking motivation. Had my faith life and practices become a ritual? It seemed that way. I was just as caught up in polarization as the next person. While there were other polarizations occurring during that time even caused by issues the church should have been truthfully addressing, there were also personal issues that we had no choice but to acknowledge.

Another distraction that permeated aspects of the pandemic was the LGTBQ movement. While many Christians outwardly attacked anyone in the movement most forgot that love is the foundation of our faith. No, I do not agree with the lifestyle. No, I will not be bullied because of another's choice just like I will not bully them because of my faith. Pastor Jerome Lewis of Seeds of Greatness Bible Fellowship put it so eloquently. He said that we are not against people. We are pro-Bible. And being pro-Bible commands me to love with agape love. So many will not allow love to be the foundation for all. And who are we to love? The Samaritan which represents whoever you think is askew from your faith. Selah...

MAKING SENSE OF TRAGEDY

This was the hardest time in my life for comfort. Many were dying for several reasons often connected to if not caused by COVID-19. Often there were senseless deaths. I cannot attack a person's faith convictions. But if I allow all to speak of faith in their own understanding, I will also allow error instead of argument. So, I began looking for answers in the Bible. Many of my answers were found in prophecy. With all that was occurring I found Matthew 24 very enlightening. While people flocked to Revelation and tried to saddle up the horses of the Apocalypse, I was asking the Holy Spirit for guidance.

I stated in a previous book titled *"The Community of We"* how the culture of fear profits from the culture of fear. This was certainly the case during the pandemic. Price gouging all the way down to fighting over things in stores was rampant. My wife told me that she had a dream that we would have to stock up canned goods and other things. She was a tad perturbed with me that I did not run out and purchased inordinate amounts of canned goods. What I did not say is that I had a terribly similar dream twice almost immediately before she had hers. And I still hold a prophetic word from the past that agreed with her dream. However, the timing was off. I am sure with some of her vocal dissention she was not interested in what I saw. Sometimes one must stand the ground that God told you to stand on. Long story short, I am glad I did not look at the visions and dreams as fearful, but as wisdom of the future.

I stated earlier how we were exposed and infected in the latter part of November 2019. We were secure in our food and shelter. But others were panicking! I recall going to the base commissary to purchase just a few in between items. I witnessed people throwing blows over chicken wings and toilet paper. I still do not know the rationale behind toilet paper to this day. Another woman in our community was with me as I made my way to the dried beans and rice. While everyone was at the "chicken" part of the display for fisticuffs and wings, I was at the smoked meat, sausage, and bacon scraps areas. Then it was off to the flour and oil section. Finally, I arrived at the canned goods section and selectively purchased what was needed. All of this was accomplished while they were still going through the brackets to find out who would be the champion of thrown hands in the meat section. And of course, there was price gouging to add to the turmoil.

One of the earliest concerns that I had was for the Marshallese people that I encountered in late February and early March of 2020. I was in Arkansas during that time to observe a solemn Day of Remembrance to the Marshallese people as them leaving their home islands because the American Government convinced (tricked) them to leave with a promise of return that has never been fully accomplished. Because of their culture being a heavy family and clan connection, they were subject to much of the virus running rampant through their community. Also, a wrongfully enacted bill had attached to it the removal of governmental medical aid to them for the damage done by the atomic weapon testing. So, everyone that passed on was funeralized in public of sorts with familial and community gatherings which furthered the spread. I was saddened because I know their love as people! I broke out in tears as I met one of their pastors who has a humble and fatherly spirit; Pastor Heam of the Seventh Day Adventist Church in Arkansas. They even embraced us as victims with them as we were those sent to clean up the radiation on many islands. It was a futile attempt. And now I am witnessing them being destroyed again by a virus.

Ironically, the day before I was flying out to Arkansas, I went to visit my brother-in-love at a specialized care facility. The drive was about forty-five minutes long to arrive. In less than forty minutes the visitation policy changed. When I arrived, the doors were locked! I must have really looked alarmed. The receptionist let me in and told me that they were on lockdown because of COVID-19. Just that quick they locked everything down! And this was no two-month endeavor! It was months before the virus did enter and began to affect everyone. But it was nowhere near other facilities. My brother-in-law eventually contracted the virus due to closed quarters. But he was spared because of the preparations and safeguards placed.

I was truly blessed even though I had driven ninety minutes round trip only to not have a visit. I was able to visit him other times during the pandemic which made it not as alarming in this area. He contracted the virus even after vaccinations. Yet, he did not die from the virus or complications, nor did he stay hospitalized for a long time during that era.

The next tragedy was of a faithful man in my community that touched my life as a youth in Washington, DC. He chose to attend a conference where the congregation began spreading the virus. Many were defiant of government directives and suffered. This was a case in which I was hurt deeply! This man opened the door for me to be a Boy Scout (that is a story with many humorous accounts) along with a man of God in the community. And he left this earth without leaving the hospital or having family (to my knowledge) around him.

Ironically, his family did not know the impact he had on people. When he left for the Air Force we were still getting into the Boy Scouts. But he opened the door for us. He was a quiet and powerful person to me even before I reconnected to him and discovered his faith. He was another person that saddened me because he followed the messages of leadership to this end. He led by example.

While a son in ministry did not die from COVID, I was at his memorial as COVID-19 really took hold in the United States. I witnessed so many churches and pastors making unwise declarations and exhorting their congregants NOT to take precautions and to defy governmental directives which is totally against the Word of God. Once I heard of the impending quarantine I returned home quickly. And those who gave such crazy directives began having illnesses, hospitalizations, and death. While many boasted of the "victory" over COVID I asked at what cost. The answer is Long COVID where they are still seeing the results of being attacked by COVID-19. It especially attacked the lungs and other organs instead of just a few weeks of illness. An associate of mine in the medical field contracted the virus. He was still suffering from breathing issues six months later. He told me that he would remember this when caring for those with COVID-19.

Not even two complete months later a young pastor close to my heart died. He had been very vocal about denying the danger of the virus and determined he would never mask or quarantine. Sadly, he contracted the virus and infected his wife. Both were hospitalized. His wife was discharged after some days. He transitioned and was alone as he died as many were in the beginning of this.

I was devastated. I begged him to at least mask which he refused constantly. I briefly got to speak with him about two days before his death. It was very, very short because he could hardly breathe! He told me to tell everyone I knew that this was nothing to play with. Then he died. I was hurt and angry because he believed the millions of social media posts and political leaders spouting that the virus was not dangerous. He is survived by his loving widow who happened to be a health care worker.

It was a dual reality moment, death, and restricted life with an alternative of death.

In 2021 we were dispatched to the Marshallese Embassy to deliver a work of art to the Marshallese people expressing a sentiment on the United States using their land as a nuclear testing ground. While there were many memorable moments during that visit the pinnacle of the visit was reuniting with Terrance Graham an Enewetak Atoll Radiation Cleanup Veteran who had been assigned to the Marshall Islands as well. He joined us there. During our conversations he stated many things that I treasured. He later died unexpectedly, and his body was not found for close to if not more than six weeks. But, even during all this caution we attended his memorial. Again, the masks were on, and precautions were taken. It was a dual reality moment, death, and restricted life with an alternative of death.

It was at that moment that I realized our polarization of behavior was programmed. In all honesty I should have been one programmed against all the precautions. Yet, I obeyed gladly. And I never had the question of whether Terrance did die by heart attack or was it COVID-related with the heart like the young pastor who died of cardiac arrest while hospitalized with COVID. Either way a dear friend was no longer with us.

In retrospect one thing that I have come to understand is this has worked together for good according to God's purpose.

In conclusion to this chapter, I still cannot make sense of the tragedy in all ways. But with requests to the Lord, I am seeing how His hand moved during this as I progress in obedience and trust. It may never make sense to me on this side of eternity. Yet there are many things that made sense many years after the event, even decades. This is where my faith and trust met the test. I just must embrace and own the truth that His thoughts are not my thoughts, nor are His ways my ways. In retrospect one thing that I have come to understand is this has worked together for good according to God's purpose. It forced many outside of their ritualistic operation and tradition to truly grasp the frailty of human life and forced them to deal outside of a building to many who do not believe the same. Illness and death hit everyone.

POLARIZATION OF BELIEVERS

Even prior to the pandemic believers were polarizing over too many issues. Bible versions, doctrine over the verbal expressions of baptism, refusal to embrace neighbors, it did not matter. We were all at odds with the odds themselves. The spirit of blame divided those who were supposed to be united. For the first time in my life, I witnessed total disrespect toward the office of the President of the United States among other vile and disrespectful actions. This was not limited to one administration but a few. Most of America and I would venture to say the vast majority do not pray for those in authority! Instead, they disrespect them. And then we wonder why we do not live in peace according to the Word of God. It is because we as a country allowed dishonor to sneak in under the guise of feigned righteousness. Those two cannot co-exist.

Now, in no way am I ignoring those who are just blatantly unrighteous and doing evil deeds. There are those elected leaders who use their elected position as a personal tool to do things that are not ethical and even illegal. Identify them. Allow the system (if it is not broken) to deal with them. Then replace them with viable and honorable leaders.

The vast majority of America and I would venture to say the vast majority do not pray for those in authority!

There was a period immediately preceding COVID where many Christian leaders labeled "evangelicals" began making statements about the President of that administration and saying he was God's choice. I beg to differ. He was a man whom God allowed and ordained for a specific time to be in power for a specific purpose if he did not attempt to steal the glory that only belongs to God. And we must remember that God will give humanity what we (collectively) want in government. He did it with Saul. That purpose could very well have been to effect major change which was and still is needed. But, like any other human on this earth, free will is present. While God may allow someone based on our own actions, He will also remove that person if they stray from His purpose or dishonor Him in any way.

If this had anything to do with Christ, then I have a brontosaurus that can tightrope walk across Niagara Falls with flip flops.

I have witnessed those who threaten another sibling in Christ with going to hell if they did not support this foolery! And you DARE NOT blame this on one President or Administration in the United States. Just as any other issue that is now a "volume," it began in the lowest form and was allowed to grow. Rarely does the population get it right in pinpointing when a disturbing trend begins. And daily polarization continues exacerbating the situation.

First there was the incident in Charlottesville, Virginia with the "alt right" marching through town during an authorized march. This was considered a "Christian" thing foundationally according to many in the "movement." If this had anything to do with Christ, then I have a brontosaurus that can tightrope walk across Niagara Falls with flip flops.

I was asked during a panel what I thought of this. I replied that I am glad it happened. The gasps that followed did not surprise me. Only one person on the panel asked me to explain my statement without prejudice. I stated emphatically that I was extremely glad that this event happened. I did not see any of this "behavior" up to eight years prior. Many thought that racism was a done deal after the election of President Barak Obama. I begged to differ. Just because an African American president was elected did not reject all of racism nor correct the centuries of injustice. It only went underground.

I told my son that while stationed in the Army paratroopers had a saying. They would proudly state that paratroopers do not die. They just go to hell and regroup. I told my son that for the last four years nothing has been voiced in opposition. If we did not hear much in 2012 then 2016 was going to be a doozie. It was. And, then the march in 2017 and the violence that ensued captured our attention.

I continued my explanation that the ones marching was authorized and orderly initially. I was not concerned about them marching through town peacefully. I wanted to know who had the bright idea to authorize it in an area known for questionable practices. It just proved that they were in some dark corner regrouping to reappear.

The elderly and seasoned panelist smiled at the observation and stated that it was truly clear what I stated. Yet this was not the clearest point that I wanted to make concerning division. It is the point that regardless of truth, transparency, and historical accountability many refuse to acknowledge that our God is a God of accountability, mercy, and truth. Yet, He has never forced us into anything that we did not wish to do.

> ***Our polarizations only enabled the enemy to continually form a wedge between us.***

And now the new divisive point is for loving our neighbor who is not who we identify as Christian. There is a myriad of theological, social, sexual, and racial differences that are not important if we name the name of Christ as our Lord and Savior. It seems as if we want to quilt patch our beliefs to justify our biases for justification of our mindset. It is wrong.

Our polarizations only enabled the enemy to continually form a wedge between us. And if we do not return fully to God it will continue to force us apart. Somehow, we tend to forget that Christ said, our "neighbor" was a "Samaritan;" that person that represents everything that is contrary to our comfortable belief system and existence.

THE DISCUSSION OF LIFE AND RIGHTS

Recently the argument of whether America is a Christian nation or not has risen again. I am of the mindset that America was founded on Judeo-Christian principles but not a Christian country. We have a Christian identifying population. Yet we are not all Christian even if we are in a majority.

Mankind can be such fools at times.

So, we were having all sorts of arguments on many topics. Race, sexuality, religion, and nation of birth were all hot topics. While I identify as a practicing Christian disciple (emphasis on disciple), there are those who have called me all manner of heretic or heathen. Why? They voiced their warped beliefs because I choose to respect every person (neighbor) on this earth regardless of whether we agree completely or not. If there is mutual respect and honor, then we have no problem. But it must be a mutual exchange.

Just as with anything there must be truth for a lie to be born.

While the virus was rapidly spreading and mutating many were blaming other nationalities and various cultures for it. I heard many attempting to blame minorities because of a refusal to be vaccinated. I can understand some hesitation seeing the United States has often used questionable practices toward minorities. But that was not the case. Then there were the patriots as they named themselves attempting to paint any medical news and possibilities as a conspiracy theory. Mankind can be such fools at times.

I arrived at the conclusion that America thrives on the blame game.

I was surprised that even a subgrouping of who I think were cognitively deficient individuals attempted to blame the LGBTQ community for the virus. And just as the media reported on it, they ended it. Of course, other conspiracy theories arose to place blame and guilt on others. Just as with anything there must be truth for a lie to be born.

I arrived at the conclusion that America thrives on the blame game. I am sure it began well before the Salem Witch Trials. Whenever something disturbs the warped peace of various individuals, they will find a way to place blame someplace or someone. There was no difference in this situation.

Where did I fit in with these blames and discussions of life and rights? I do not know. But I do know that I could have been in a couple of categories of blame as I listened to all the excitement about COVID-19, the ineffective vaccine and how "those people" are the super spreaders.

We all had episodes of exposure regardless of how careful you were. I was no different. I am sure I was exposed numerous times. However, it was my choice to seek out and get the vaccine not to be a guinea pig as many were saying "we" who chose the vaccine were. I chose it because I did not want to be the carrier who it may not have affected to someone in a risk group who was not vaccinated costing them their life! To me it was a no brainer. I waited until capitalism produced competition for the market and watched the results. I did not want to bring the virus home or take it anywhere else for that matter as I have seen in other cases.

I did not do this because I had a lack of faith or fear. I have a respect for the Corona virus. I did it because since I love my neighbor as myself, I will do everything to keep both safe and healthy. And I did it because I love my family and friends. I did not want them to see me suffer. And I surely never want to see them suffer. But while I was standing firm on my convictions there were others who had convictions of a cockroach when it came to their perceived violation of rights.

People were refusing to wear surgical or other masks that would protect them as well as the population from the spreading of the virus. I will be the first to bemoan the difficulty of breathing when you are masked and with sinus congestion. The mask robbed me of the extra air I needed to endure the mucus! It was a pain in the posterior for me! Yet, I did it without complaint. Some were purposely not wearing protective equipment and coughing intentionally without covering up. I even watched a few physical confrontations because of masking. It would have been such a peaceful resolution if they either separated or just masked. But often people want to result in physical violence, which is normally a sign of removed self-esteem, fear or just ignorance being masked by manipulation.

Then something wonderful happened. I began meeting people with the same convictions as me. Political parties normally were not the factor. But we all shared a need to show the love of Christ by looking out for our neighbor. This is where I began to see more hope from society.

OPTIONS

What was prevalent at the beginning of the pandemic was the lack of options. Many congregations never planned for the possible situation that would preclude anyone attending worship in person. This was confined to the sick and shut in list. While many churches already streamed live worship services, some were determined to keep the ministry off the "hell-a-vision" with all that worldly sin situated around the same channels. Then the pandemic closed their doors.

Everyone had a word from the Lord concerning the pandemic and the ensuing deaths.

Another option that presents itself is the internet and various applications to stream. Facebook was an extremely popular platform for many ministries. And then again there were ministries being "birthed" because of the pandemic. Everyone had a word from the Lord concerning the pandemic and the ensuing deaths. Just as with the AIDS epidemic there were those that wanted to tie the pandemic to some perceived sin or collection of sins from America.

Suddenly every sin that could be identified was assigned some hierarchical value depending on the sin. Certainly, according to many, homosexuality is the worst thing a person could do while being followed close second place and almost tying the ranking by murder. But there were those who had hidden desires for a myriad of things that were made manifest during the pandemic.

I was personally shocked by a mentee that had hidden a desire for quite some time only for it to break out full force during the pandemic. I was called on to intervene with various individuals who were addicted to substances or actions. It was surreal to see this unfold right before my eyes, oftentimes concerning individuals who hid the issue so well. Some who were considered the crème of the crop began coming to me in super-privacy to ask for guidance and prayer for things they may have been involved in for some time. However, the pandemic brought these hidden things to the top of observation.

In a previous work I penned that I supported a candidate for an elected governmental position; a person that was an openly gay married man. He was very qualified for the position. But as with the pandemic there were those that wanted to apply Bible verses *selectively* to justify some of their bigotry. They used portions of verses to justify their choice or lack of choice of a candidate. When asked why, I would only answer the obvious. The Constitution never stated anything concerning a person's sexual orientation or religion. Yet, many were determined to state that America was founded on the Bible and a Christian nation. It is not. That was one of the reasons for many to come to America, religious freedom among many other "freedoms" that dare not be attempted in other countries.

Additional options included denominational choices. Methodism was under fire because of doctrinal choices being made concerning the LGBTQ community. The denomination of the African-Methodist Episcopalians remained firm in their doctrine of not ordaining or marrying openly gay couples. But as with any organization they had flaws in other areas. The Southern Baptists took a lot of criticism from their stances on minorities and women which shouldn't have come as a shock. When doctrine begins to be questioned often the denomination tries to justify the thought process of the dissent. While in my observation many of the questioning revolves around money, lately they include many things such as women in leadership and other female gender-related issues.

While I am not opposed to a woman in leadership, I am opposed to men who belittle them.

When the pandemic hit, I never thought I would see so many people concerned about women pastors. While I am not opposed to a woman in leadership, I am opposed to men who belittle them. Scripture plainly states that there is no difference between believers. Additionally, it is proven that women were apostles as well. But this is not to say that all the titled apostles in Christendom are true apostles. Yet I do not have the time, energy, resources, or desire to run down every person with a title and test their legitimacy. There are enough Christians that think their calling is to be God's Enforcers and Tithe Collectors, the Holy Ghost Storm Troopers. The Word of God tells us to work out our own salvation with fear and trembling. This means while I am concentrating on my own walk, I will not have time to judge yours.

> *There are enough Christians that think their calling is to be God's Enforcers and Tithe Collectors, the Holy Ghost Storm Troopers.*

The final two options are taken often. The first one of staying home and streaming across the internet because of the fear of contracting some illness has overtaken many. Regardless of any new statistics, many will feed the fear demon and stay at home to escape germs. Yet, these very same people will host huge gatherings at their home and invite many people with no protection. Many use excuses such as family get togethers or "fellowship" meetings at home. We wrongly test God by doing what we think we should do without consulting Him as instructed in Proverbs 3:5,6. Sadly, this was the case with many in my community. They attempted to tie in the restrictions of the pandemic with persecution. There was no comparison, only a desire to justify rebellion against the law.

The final option that has been taken more than we think is to just not attend any worship service anywhere with anyone. This has been the most justified option for many. The age-old adage that we do not have to come to a building to worship the Lord has taken a crooked turn and rooted again. But this idea has always been in the forefront of what many tried to justify concerning church attendance and absence. No, we do not have to come to a specific building to worship the Lord. Yet we do need to gather to be a congregation of disciples to be effective. But since congregations often only gather at a building designated as a church or worship center this is the only place where many think they can come to experience God.

I have witnessed God show up at a bar when the messenger was sent.

I can say that I have experienced God in places where others think I had no business even thinking

God would show up there and much less show His glory. I can speak unequivocally that if God directs you to a place for a purpose, He will already be there waiting for you. And this place does not have to be a church building.

I have witnessed God show up at a bar when the messenger was sent. The person the messenger was sent to was me. I can recall that shock just like it was yesterday. And, to top it off the individual had not been living in the city for over a week. He was just obedient to God and walked in the bar to deliver a personalized message for me. It shocked me so bad that I sobered up instantly; I mean like a wave of sobriety swept over me. When he left, I tried to regain my tipsy demeanor to no avail. I had been touched by the hand of God. So even if there are people that refuse to come back to a building, God will dispatch servants to them. He has done this more than once with me.

One such incident happened when I was visiting the Veterans Administration clinic. This little grandmotherly lady stopped me at the elevator and called me out to the Lord as to who I was and what I was to be doing. She was correct in what she said. I had never seen this woman before in my life. Her husband is also a powerful man of God. Before it was over there was a line for prayer at the elevator with some men saying they were waiting for their prayers. This is another instance of God sending people to perform His will even if we act tone deaf to His direction. Sadly, he has transitioned to heaven early in 2025. He is missed greatly.

A view to consider for those who think that the "Way" just grew with no opposition is recorded in Chapter 2 of the Book of Acts. If the people stayed in the synagogue there was no problem! The moment they began going from house to house, breaking bread, then persecution and CHURCH GROWTH ensued, making the church grow rapidly.

But first they had to get out of the building/synagogue. I keep remembering the one line that I removed from "The Community of We", *God would allow something to force us out of the building to fully touch the community and its residents.* Again, work out your own salvation. There will be enough fear and trembling as we see others melting with fear because they are inundated with media news and internet articles.

In the Book of Revelation, it is recorded that the "water" from the dragon's mouth was trying to sweep away the "man child" that the woman was protecting. Prophetically water can symbolize information. The man child represents an ever-learning being that will try to ingest all the information coming to him. I submit to you that the enemy understands that ignorance can destroy people. But that is the lack of knowledge. Too much knowledge can also be dangerous. I am a specialist in rabbit hole exploration! I must stay focused on completing the task at hand. Otherwise, I will have a lot of information without any ability to apply the information.

I can say that too much information can be even more detrimental than not enough. If we view our minds and brains as computers as the Lord intended, then we would understand that we can be overloaded and crash. This is the problem with total access to information floating around on the web. Yet we all want access to the information without having checks and balances.

King Agrippa had the right idea when he told Paul that much learning had made him mad. While Paul was full of the Holy Spirit, King Agrippa thought that his boldness came from his numerous years of academic and theological training. This can be the same today concerning those operating under the anointing of God. It may appear that they are a tad off center in their rocker. Yet God still works in mysterious ways. His thoughts are not our thoughts. Nor are His ways our ways. I am in awe at how I see Him move in my own life. It totally amazes me at times. One of the main ways He moves in my life is to have me pray for others, especially those who have done, wish to do or are doing me wrong in the present or have wronged me in the past. As we obey this directive of the Lord something begins to happen. You begin to "feel" empathy and sympathy for the individuals. This is what graduate faith is all about.

THE FRUIT OF THE PANDEMIC

The pandemic produced much fruit (and a few nuts as well) that aided in our solitude. So many things happened during the pandemic. First there was the boom in pet adoption and purchasing. So many individuals supplemented their emotional outlets by purchasing or adopting pets. It was nothing to see people walking dogs throughout the housing community at regular intervals. People that I would have thought would never own a dog suddenly had two and a slew of gerbils. It was a good day for the dog or cat awaiting adoption. But in the end the animals became an unexpected burden. Many are now returning to the shelter arrangements with hopes of a more permanent and thought-out adoption.

I already owned two dogs that were family: a father and son. They could zero in on what was going on with their humans. The father and I shared a remarkably close bond. He was with me for many issues that involved surgery or bedrest. His son is a quirky fellow that will run like he has been scalded if he does not understand something. Sadly, the day after Christmas 2021 we had to put the father to his heavenly sleep. That really wrecked me. He held on until I was mobile from orthopedic surgery. Then he could not stand. I was an emotional wreck taking him to the emergency veterinarian.

For a second, they were not going to let me be with him as he transitioned. I was not having it. I was fully prepared to take my dog home with me and let him die in familiar surroundings with familiar people. They allowed me to be out back in the cold with him as he drifted off. His eyes sparkled as he saw his human being holding him as he slipped into bliss. Even now I am almost ready to tear up.

Something funny happened after this. The son took on a completely different personality after his father did not return with the humans. It took a month before he would go out the front door or get into the vehicle though. All he knew was that Daddy never came back. He eventually grieved in his own way by being ultra clingy to me. Now he is like an appendage since he is always at my side. He even took a turn for the better during the pandemic. His attentiveness improved along with his social skills. He was always a tad standoffish. Now he is much more social yet observant. And he enjoys being the only recipient of treats and belly rubs. But I still miss his dad.

> **Marriage was returning to a time past when husband and wife were constantly in each other's presence.**

Many relationships took a different approach to the pandemic. I was surprised to discover that many couples divorced because of the pandemic and the proximity of life quarantined. Then I took an introspective look at my own marriage. While we were married, we often had escapes from employment, social functions, and many other avenues to not be in constant proximity to the other. Now we were resigned to the fact that we needed to "like" one another and to accept those quirks that we normally would not see in each other. Now they were staring at us in the face. A whole new life was about to begin behind quarantined doors. Marriage was returning to a time past when husband and wife were constantly in each other's presence.

Sometimes the mirror that we must gaze into has a different face but the same behaviors that you dislike, behaviors like your own.

One of the first things that I noticed was that my priority schedule was not like my wife's. While I was content cooking and cleaning dishes later, she was determined to clean as she (or I) went. She was heavily on my last and most exposed nerve. Then there was the criticism of whether something was done differently. The humor in it was that I had been doing it the way she observed for quite a while. She just was not around to comment on it. Now, she saw it all. And I saw all of hers as well. Sometimes the mirror that we must gaze into has a different face but the same behaviors that you dislike, behaviors like your own.

During this time, I focused on humility.

So, the fruit that I harvested from this isolated solitude that was forced upon many because of the pandemic was sweet and bitterly sour. It was sweet because I had the opportunity to gaze into my own shortcomings and become humble. During this time, I focused on humility. I wanted to see where I could improve. So, I focused on those things I had "conquered" to see if I had truly overcome them.

People that would normally never speak to one another began interacting on personal levels.

The number one thing was my tongue! That piece of flesh can be something to control. It cannot and will not be tamed. Yet it can be controlled. I discovered that I needed to control it more even in the face of verbal lashings. It was even more important for me to control it during those moments because I could unleash a counterattack in a New York minute that could wound a spirit, wreck a soul, and devastate destinies. I had to acknowledge that discipline was needed in this situation. To be brutally honest, this is one of the main things that I must keep under subjection constantly. There was a season when I was a well-practiced and qualified vulgarian with a razor-sharp wit.

Relationships were forced into a forge. People that would normally never speak to one another began interacting on personal levels. Again, I recall the couple that I met at the Veterans Administration. Their Christian convictions were so strong until I was wondering if they may even scare off help that God was sending because they did not speak in tongues. But they did not scare anyone away. In fact, they began to interact with a couple that lived a different lifestyle than they approved of. During this time acceptance of the person became the primary focus along with staying healthy. While the neighbors did not live a Christian lifestyle, they had moral values that were conducive to the faith of my friends to a certain point. Often those whom we walk away from frowning with disdain are the exact same ones that God may be sending. Too often we wish to be God and design what we think is best. Well apart from God man has attempted to do that for a few millenniums. How has that been working out for us?

Then there is the necessary destruction of religious stereotypes. The pandemic brought destruction upon all cultures and religions. It did not respect anyone's faith, race, sexuality, or political affiliation. It showed us that we have humanity with the imminent appointment with death in common. While I am a firm believer that we all have a date assigned to us, we can also quicken our own demise. This was the situation with COVID-19. Many attempted to tout their immunity and invincibility in the face of the virus. Some did not prevail as they thought.

A very bright spot in this dark cloud was who was considered essential during this time. A closer look was given to those "lowly" workers who were still required to work. It gave humanity a needed boost to stimulate mutual respect and dignity. My heart would sink at the way some people treated those working in the big box stores or even grocery stores. I have always said in the military that if you want to find out who really keeps things moving, send all the privates and low-ranking people home. The same principle applied here. And even with this truth being evident in the faces of those who thought they were so important there were still those who wanted to disrespect these workers that were waiting on them for their needs.

The home health care aides were on the front lines. So many health care workers rose to the clarion call until I was in awe at the nurses that I personally knew. We saw heroes in action, but they did not wear capes. I am profoundly grateful to the health care workers who cared for my brother-in-love while he was in a skilled care facility. They were awesome in their carefulness. During this time, I had home visits from physical therapy and occupational therapy. I respected them for their dedication to the patients assigned. Yet, I am sure many had no idea these people were still on the front lines witnessing the damage caused by a virus.

One thing that I did treasure during this period was the connection made with a new neighbor that had moved immediately preceding COVID-19 from another state. My grandson and my neighbor's son connected eye gazes during a walk. I admire how children have no prejudice or bias. They just connect and keep moving to the next fun activity. During the pandemic, the husband and I did quite a bit of fishing and crabbing. He was from a plains state yet taught me how to crab! They taste so much better when they are caught and free of cost. His name spoke volumes concerning him. His name is Chance.

We always discussed the Bible in context and how it touches individual lives or applied to our own life.

I think I will wreck some people's theology now. Chance is a Mormon. His life is his testimony. The man knew nothing of me nor my situation (I was recovering from various maladies including being rearended at a traffic stop). He was eager to help anyone in the community in any fashion. His life exemplified the life and testimony of a Christian man. Yet when I mentioned him the first thing many Christians heard was "he is a Mormon." And this question never came up unless they pressed to know where he "fellowshipped" or where was he a "member" of. Any theological discussion we had never centered on The Book of Mormon or The Pearl of Great Price or any other commentary of Protestantism of which many were on my shelves. We always discussed the Bible in context and how it touches individual lives or applied to our own life.

You would have thought that I brought Hannibal Lector to a surgeon's conference with a fresh bottle of hot sauce.

I mentioned to another brother in Christ that my neighbor and I were spending time together fishing, crabbing, and just goofing off some. He gave me a semi-veiled interrogation concerning who, what, when, where, and why this man could be close. I was getting perturbed with his demanding interview. Then I mentioned in his faith questioning that he was a Mormon. You would have thought that I brought Hannibal Lector to a surgeon's conference with a fresh bottle of hot sauce.

When I mentioned the warped encounter to Chance, he told me of something that happened with his employment. One of the people asked him if he was Mormon how many wives he had? Chance is a quick thinker. So, he told him that he had six and came to the new assignment to find a Sunday wife. I would have loved to have seen the expression on the guy's face. Chance has this clandestine sense of humor where you can be bleeding and not knowing he cut you.

While I was familiar with some aspects of the Mormon faith, we connected on the fact of the death, burial, and resurrection of Jesus the Christ; and crabbing or fishing of course. His wife baked things that were sinfully heavenly. I believe she could go out into the yard, pull up poison ivy, bake it, and make it heavenly. I adored the kids and even the new addition who is such a pleasant baby. Yet I knew that they must leave soon. It was for this departure that I waited to finish this work among other possible reasons. For some reason there were difficulties and delays popping up with the completion of this work. I did not get angry. Instead, I inquired of the Lord to see what my next direction would be.

While I have learned through life to be prepared and in expectation for unexpected connections, others are often stubbornly horrified concerning new connections.

One thing is certain, the pandemic forced us to connect to those on earth that we may never have sought out connections with. While I have learned through life to be prepared and in expectation for unexpected connections, others are often stubbornly horrified concerning new connections. While we are on this earth, we must be constantly aware that God never had a cookie cutter when He began disbursing humans across the earth. We come in many sizes, shapes, hues, temperaments, and purposes. Yet we tend to search out at all costs for those with every aspect of their lives identical to ours. BORING! There are some lifestyles that I have no inkling to discover or live. Yet, there are others that I would like to try, but not permanently.

Chance remained with us while the family transitioned to a new location. I had the joy of having him under the same roof periodically even though his former employer was working him like a Hebrew in Egypt. Just in casual conversation I could tell that he was very proficient in his field. So, I understand that his previous employer needed to squeeze the last semi-damp drop of blood from him before he let him escape!

He introduced me to his father who came to visit. We all enjoyed fishing and crabbing, catching nothing. Once Chance told me about a situation with his father, I began to immediately pray that he could be closer to his father. God answered the prayer. He found a job close to his father and placed his house on the market. It sold in forty-eight hours.

While his family moved home, he returned to tie up loose ends in the area. Once the statement was made of his temporary choices for lodging, we knew it was not to be. He had full access to the home and everything else that we had. There was never a question of "if" but "when."

Either way, there will always be those who can find a negative outlook while being totally blessed by God.

I did experience negativity from select associates that may have either witnessed his unrestricted access to my residence or heard me speak of a wonderful house guest. Either way, there will always be those who can find a negative outlook while being totally blessed by God. But I will say that such input assisted me in tightening my circle of access.

We all have biases of something, people, places, and things.

It was during the pandemic and the ensuing isolation that others began allowing their inner biases to surface. We all have biases of something, people, places, and things. Yet, if we totally surrender to the task of displaying agape (decisional) love in all situations, we will confront these biases that we recognize in our own lives. I certainly began noticing quirks in my own philosophy of life. And they were not pretty! Many mornings I gazed into the mirror and wondered where "that" thought came from. Yet we often do not address these disturbing thoughts because we can hide in the abyss of our "existence" apart from those things which make us biased.

He is a man of God regardless of who may wish to judge.

While I missed the whole family, I did have Chance to converse with upon occasion as he would happen through between shifts of making bricks with no straw. Upon his departure he left me a card which I will treasure eternally. I did not realize he was that observant (at least in the aspect of me operating in faith and charity). While I was ensuring that I did not leave my socks lying on the floor by my favorite reclining TV chair he was watching my passion for sustainable and impactful missions overseas. In fact, he was a missionary with the Church of Latter-Day Saints in his younger years. I learned a lot from his training and experiences, as I am sure he did from mine. He is a man of God regardless of who may wish to judge.

His wonderful wife, Shuan, is the epitome of mothers. As she explained the selection and choice for missionary within the Latter-Day Saints doctrine, it was explained that the calling of motherhood is above all. I agree since I see the maladies from absent parents, especially mothers. It is this very first relational connection that shapes the life of the child for societal life. I could think of no other woman that I could point to for such an example at this time. She is educated, gifted, experienced and an example of true agape love to everyone. Yet, her calling as a mother superseded everything else.

Chance and Shuan are friends beyond life, not just neighbors or associates.

They were angels sent to show us that God always has His eye on us and help is close. Chance and Shuan are friends beyond life, not just neighbors or associates. They would always check on us as we would with them. Certainly, the children won my heart. Joyce politely let me know that I had purchased deficient Gummi Worms (I tried to cut corners for convenience).

Curtis is quite a jokester, always making me laugh. He stole my heart the first time we were fishing. He fell in the water (albeit shallow). I witnessed his mother without any effort "levitate" and grabbed him from the water! He was more shocked than anything else. I asked him if he went swimming. With his mischievous grin and shivering body, he said, "uh huh"! I miss that little guy! And eventually the arrival of Connor, the most pleasant child I have ever seen! I am sure Connor will test the limits eventually since he is the youngest of the tribe.

During this time, I had a hip replacement as well. With advances made because of the pandemic, I was hospitalized overnight. I remember making a comment that childbirth mothers stayed in the hospital longer than me. I never had to worry at all. Before I could get out of my modified recliner and cook (I love to work in the kitchen over) Chance's wife would show up with creations for a king (and the sweets that would nocturnally disappear). She is wholeheartedly responsible for me returning to eat cookies in the middle of the night just in case the cookie monster showed up and wanted to criminally remove her cookies. With my total dedication and due diligence no cookies were stolen by the cookie monster! And I still am vigilant for his unwelcome arrival. I do have regrets that I never finished piano lessons with her. Pandemic life had a way of turning heads in other directions. She would have conversations concerning worship and hymns. I can appreciate her love for older hymns. She had a passion for those songs of worship that were considered sacred. I do agree that we cannot allow some worship to slip away. I listen to lyrics today and wonder what Gospel they are lending melody to.

It is times like the pandemic that will test the mettle of your faith and dedication.

These are just select few windows to peer into the pandemic. I had to almost meditate on Romans

8:28 continuously. All of this is working together for the purposes of God. That does not mean that we are going to be comfortable. But it is all in His purpose and plan. And, as I live and remember the events of the era, I can see that regardless of what I saw God was working it in our favor and for HIS purpose.

It was during this time that I had to take full inventory of my Christianity and discipleship.

It is times like the pandemic that will test the mettle of your faith and dedication. It was during this time that I had to take full inventory of my Christianity and discipleship. I discovered that what many called Christianity was nothing more than a set of practices and chronological rituals linked to a religious belief that could be held loosely or tightly to one's spirit. I thank COVID-19 for this opportunity. You see if there is no pressure there can be no measurement. If the is no measurement, there can be no progress. And, if there is no progress you are stagnant. This was all accomplished in the pandemic.

SPRITUAL LONG COVID

I read on more instances that the effects of Long COVID-19 on patients linger and even causing more discomfort than the onset of the virus. I submit to you that we suffer from a spiritual Long COVID as well. While we were overjoyed at the possibility of being able to assemble again, there were those who were content rallying the household congregation (and not continuous) in front of the electronic pulpit. I stated earlier that my nephew with family in tow would awaken, perform all aspects of hygiene and dressing, go downstairs, and begin to worship as if they were in a church with other congregants. But I would be the first to tell you that his family not only weathered the pandemic but grew exponentially both spiritually and socially. Practices like these caught my eye and kept my attention.

We are often sidetracked concerning tradition instead of revelation and development.

On the other hand, there were those who would fight a platoon of rabid dragons to keep "tradition" alive. I remember once a member of the family upon hearing news of my relocation had only one question. Where would we have our holiday? Nothing else seemed to matter even though there were many open locations of family members' homes and other locations. But the tradition overrode everything else in their eyes. This is the same as we do in church. We are often sidetracked concerning tradition instead of revelation and development.

The period of 2021 to the present time frame has been one filled with pains and unexpected tragedies. Besides the myriads of deaths related to the pandemic, I also experienced the transitions of close relationships to include relatives and friends that were considered family. Pastor Jerome Lewis stated, "you can always find out secrets at weddings and funerals." I found this to be true. In the funerals of this era so many "secrets" concerning inheritances and lineages popped out with no effort! These secrets had been held for decades for whatever reason. Normally it had to do with lineage and paternity. Yet other secrets such as backroom handshake deals on property and money happened as well. Either way things in darkness became known. Wars ensued over material possessions, old promises, and stolen property. And all of this occurs within Chrisitan families.

But as I was praying and wondering how all of this just sprang up, I felt the Lord imprinting on my heart that it did not "just happen." It has been going on for quite some time in the form of distraction, division, and cultural folly. Our distraction kept us looking at a myriad of other topics; religion, politics, cultural wokeism, pandemic issues, racial inequalities and injustice were just a few. Somehow politics became somewhat interwoven in

American society with religion. My observation is for those who name the name of Jesus and embrace His word.

The furthest I will delve at this point into "politics" is that according to *1 Timothy 2:1-2,* Paul exhorts us to pray for those in authority so we can live a peaceful life. God did not give me the option of praying for those who I like or even for ME to pick the prayer. He said for us pray for those in authority so we can live peaceful lives. This means only He can give you the ingredients of the prayer concerning this. Somehow, we have misrepresented our Lord by equating His righteousness with our desire for what we deem to be right in our own eyes. This is a grave error.

While I can never agree with all that I see in culture today, I can never disrespect those who live opposed to my faith either.

This one point alone has caused so much division until the tenacles reaching from this one talking point give the appearance of a millipede with legs spreading and moving in unison. Righteous religiosity, political extremism, White Nationalism, Black Lives Matter (Incorporation not the movement), and a slew of other organizations contribute to the confusion and difficulty of unity. Stir all these ingredients into a pot already boiling with false appeals to a supernatural third party and the toxic potion gains strength and momentum. I do not espouse either party. What I do espouse is the truth regardless of party. And neither party carries the full truth of God.

This leads us into cultural folly where everyone says and does as they want the same as in the Book of Judges. While I can never agree with all that I see in culture today, I can never disrespect those who live opposed to my faith either. This is where I differentiate myself from those who are quick to use a smidgen of Bible verse to support hatred and bigotry. You are a liar, and the truth is far from you. Yet those who attempt to use the Bible to justify deviant lifestyles are just as much liars as anyone else on the same road of damnation as others, which includes many who claim Christianity.

Culture does not form Christianity. Christianity forms culture.

There is no big transgression or inequity followed by a little sin. It is all equal; unrighteous with the required penalty being death. Culture does not form Christianity. Christianity forms culture. Yet we have allowed culture to dictate changes to the Word of God for us to fit in our own theology.

Often, we have major discrepancies with people outside our window, but not the one in the mirror.

Spiritual Long COVID is just as deadly and debilitating as viral Long COVID is in the natural world. We adjusted to fit daily routines and functions without a plan to return to normal. When the opportunity arrived for our return to normalcy most opted to remain fluid, making decisions on a cuff concerning spiritual development. What we did was to remove discipleship and replace it with "churching" or as Dr. Hart Ramsey so eloquently stated it, "we have become highly developed in church." Again, I am writing this in MY transparency. Your story may be similar or different. Either way, it will be YOUR story and not mine. But, in the meantime, I did not like what I discovered concerning me.

Often, we have major discrepancies with people outside our window, but not the one in the mirror. The standard for others is extremely high while we only want mercy for ourselves. This is not the standard that God intended for us. While we often ascribe the Lord as fair, I do not agree. I do agree that we serve a "just" God. If He were fair, He would have $10 and split it down the middle for distribution even though one need may be more than $5. But a just God will disburse the funds according to need, not equality. This is the same as we are to be just. Yet we tend to lean toward the "fair" line especially when it benefits us. This is where the downfall of many, to include myself, began.

While many became entrenched in a "habitual ritual" and the mundane "church" requirements others began to really slide down the incline into spiritual apathy. It was here where I began to wonder why I did not see the chasm between discipleship (TRUE discipleship not just buzz wording it) and churchism or what is considered today, Christianity.

It is man's nature to congregate and belong to a "group."

It has been fashionable for some time now with those who wish to identify with something larger than themselves whether social groups, sororities, fraternities, or gangs and in many cases the military. But an observation reveals that many of these same people will connect themselves to all connections to "belong." It is man's nature to congregate and belong to a "group." God even stated that it was not good for man to be alone. On earth God operates through hands, feet, mouths, and bodies that are not His own body, but part of the Body of Christ. While God will not operate in this dimension because of limiting Himself and going against His own will, He still depends on us to get things done in the earth for Him through obedience.

FIG SATIN

This is a play on words, pig Latin. When I was a student in Catholic schools as a youth some of the kids would speak "pig Latin." I never understood it. But they did. So, I did not waste time trying to learn something that would only be spoken to be deceptive around the same ones who spoke it to one another. It made as much sense as letting an agitated porcupine run through a room of inflated balloons.

As I was meditating on certain passages that came up in my spirit, I remembered the fig tree. It has been speculated that the fig tree's leaves were used to "cover" our nakedness. It is also the tree that Jesus cursed for being fruitless. So, the fig tree captured my curiosity. That is when I heard 'fig Latin.' Of course, I did not have a clue at the time what I was hearing.

But as I listened, I discovered the fig is a very hearty flower that is considered fruit by many, often growing in climate zones that everything else may die in. It is an inverted flower instead of a fruit. This also lends to the fact that we often use our own devices to hide our nakedness of sin and rebellion. But the next word; satin, caught me off guard. Why would fig go with satin?

It is within the "fig satin" mindset that we cast off discipleship which is accountability at its highest form.

Satin is comfortable, plush, inviting and captivating. So why wouldn't the fig which is used as our attempt to cover our unrighteousness along with the comfort of satin? Now, I am beginning to understand. We get extremely comfortable in our own attempt to cover our issues so much until it becomes second nature if one is not cautious. This leads to my burning desire for true discipleship, not the "you carry my bags and books" discipleship lie.

Our flower of mindset is inverted forming fruit of sorts that is peculiar and not normal.

It is within the "fig satin" mindset that we cast off discipleship which is accountability at its highest form. Our flower of mindset is inverted forming fruit of sorts that is peculiar and not normal. Even Jesus had accountability! On more than one occasion He stated that He did nothing without seeing His Father do it or say anything without hearing His Father say it first. This is the same action as a child that covers his or her eyes and says "peek-a-boo" like we cannot see them. The sad part is that we do the same concerning God with our fig satin.

It is truly a harrowing thought to me to realize whenever we sin God is sitting right in the midst watching us. I do not mean to be crude, but it lends to the thought of an unfaithful wife. The book of Hosea really took me back when I first read it! God tells His prophet, go marry a whore. She is still going to act like a whore. When she cannot deliver what she promised to other men she will be put on the auction block. And you will go buy her back and bring her home with you. You will continue to love her as if nothing happened. You are doing this because this is what I do for you all each time you deliberately leave my presence.

God watches her prepare for the night, get dressed and leave. He is with her during the transportation and every other event of the evening. Then He returns home with her in the aftermath. As a man, I cannot process this in my mind and much less emotions. While I do know of some men who have stood beside the woman while this is happening. But they are far and few in between. Yet, we treat God with this "fig satin" mentality all the while attempting to cover up our own mess, justify it while attacking others on their mess not realizing that we are "the mess." We must improve!

DISCIPLESHIP NOT DUPLICATION OF THE SAME

We are to make disciples according to the mandate of Christ. Yet somewhere in the past discipleship took a dive to collect spiritual sons and daughters, spiritual foster children in many cases. As long as the tribute flows then the connection glows. Once a question is asked or a behavior is questioned then it is off with their head! I, too, have experienced this. Yet, the Lord blessed me to be observant from a distance.

There are many that I observe from a distance. One father figure, a pastor, a foreigner of sorts has been a powerful image and example to me. In 2020 a group of veterans connected with the Marshallese people for a "Day of Remembrance" of which not many Americans know why they gather. I would challenge all Americans to learn our collective history and not just the glory days that have been selectively fed to us as students in an often-deceptive educational system. We have darkness in our history just like any other nation.

The Marshallese people were lulled off their islands with a lie concerning their faith, our faith, in the Supreme God of Abraham, Issac and Jacob. Scripture was used to have lower their guards. And for them to allow it according to God's will (I am sure they did not trust strangers) is a testament to their faith. Even now they still await a return to the promised restored land. And, every year they still say, "It's in God's hand." It tears me up even though I lied to as well and sent to clean up an impossible situation. Yet, I have gained so much from such a sad situation in all aspects of my existence.

During this time of observation, I began watching and listening to what he said. I watched his posts for his family on Facebook. I observed how he carried himself during this diaspora, being a Marshallese man that had possible genetic damage because of all the nuclear tests but at the same time had the ravages of COVID-19 arise its ugly head. I was beyond humbled to never read a cross post, see any sadness even in death and behold joy in all situations. He kept telling me that I needed Marshallese music. I am still gathering some even though I have no idea what is being said this time. But recently I was in Wisconsin and overheard a few words in Marshallese that I knew! So, Pastor Heam was/is unknowing strength to me.

I believe with all my heart that a connection to God through a legitimate and viable pastor was the determining factor in our state of wellbeing.

As stated in earlier chapters, I was really depressed from the deaths of colleagues, mentees, and friends. Not many of my personal relatives passed away from this virus. Yet, I know others who lost many family members to the virus or other virus-induced causes. I believe with all my heart that a connection to God through a legitimate and viable pastor was the determining factor in our state of wellbeing. Even though there were tense moments here, the family was grounded in the word of God and hearing it through our pastor on a continual basis.

So, in these times of turmoil there were other examples to gaze upon. There is no way that anyone can tell me that during this period they stayed the same. I would even venture to say that they noticed dismal changes in their own lives by themselves with no outside attention. I did.

Times when I would be "caught up in my feelings," I would always think of what the Marshallese people endured at the hands of America. Yet, these people are forgiving beyond the bounds that we know. I do remember the tragedy in the Amish Community of Nickel Mines in rural Pennsylvania. Everyone heralded the forgiveness of the community. Even I was amazed. Yet, I could not give them the "record" for forgiveness because I knew of the Marshallese people and their plight.

While I do not wish to compare trauma, I do wish to not limit the future effects of each.

What I am saying is that even in the worst of observations we still had examples to draw wisdom and hope from. Yes, there will always be those that will find the most pessimistic situation while being seated next to the throne of God if possible. And I would caution anyone concerned about being in the company of draining people for any amount of time. But if you ask the Holy Spirit, He will surely bring others alongside you that can hold up your arms in support.

In many cases what turned out to be a time of strengthening turned into times of discipleship.

Without realizing it I was being exposed to those who claimed they were very settled in their Christian Walk, so they professed. While I was settled in my faith, I was rattled at times. Therefore, God brought many from outside my normal exposure to strengthen me. Why did He even have to do this? He had to do it because I had begun to sink just like Peter. Many in my circles prior to the pandemic were strong if no difficulties arose. But in this situation, they were not buoyant. They were rocks.

Discipleship develops your spiritual muscles by the resistance of life while you are being conditioned to be in the image and likeness of Christ.

These same people were strategic lifesavers at different periods. Some may have given marital observational advice. Another may have given direct spiritual advice. Yet others could only give what they had which may not have been what they thought they had. In many cases what turned out to be a time of strengthening turned into times of discipleship as well.

Discipleship develops your spiritual muscles by the resistance of life while you are being conditioned to be in the image and likeness of Christ. This was no exception to me. I was being bombarded with negative things, things that were painful as well. Yet, in them all I had the proper examples to follow.

The isolation of the saints proved to be just as disrupting and deadly as anything else.

We do not think of what we have outside our window because we are too focused on the individual in the mirror wrapped in constricting emotions. The isolation of the saints proved to be just as disrupting and deadly as anything else. We forgot that cherished traditional activity called fellowship. We forgot about things such as wise counsel and accountability.

Trauma is like a pigeon. It will follow you home expecting to be fed daily.

Accountability was something that I tried to find in people (although sometimes not as diligent) to be accountable to specific individuals. I quickly found a counselor that would be real with me and not let me give myself therapy. And then I began taking inventory of my life beginning with childhood while pausing at each avenue of necessity. Trauma is real. Trauma is like a pigeon. It will follow you home expecting to be fed daily.

My first inventory was for mentors. Now mind you, mentors do not have to know they are mentoring me. I can watch you from afar just as I can when you are not a mentor. But I began taking inventory of mentors. The most prevalent one was my pastor. His was a voice that I never stopped hearing and hope never to stop hearing his voice.

The transition was made from in-person to online seamlessly. Then there was a neighbor of mine, Chance. His demeanor kept me striving to be as levelheaded as he was, especially when I knew others tried his patience. He had the patience of Job while I had the "hands" of Peter. There were others that I drew strength from in various situations, but the ones that I could see and hear constantly were the ones that made the difference. There is no doubt my wife was surely an accountability partner as well. There was no way that she would not be included on that roster even if she were not invited!

But the one person that I viewed from afar was Pastor Charles Heam. I watched as he navigated this complete pandemic visiting grandchildren and others of the Marshallese community all while remaining faithful to the Lord. I watched his worship whenever I could steal a peek online. I watched most of his family's posts online. And I watched what the responses were to such joyful posts in such a time as this. What I saw constantly was the joy of the Lord. I am sure he does not know how many times I would just stare at his picture wondering how he would handle the same situation that I was presented with. I did the same thing concerning my pastor which I have never done before concerning any other pastor. I can't say that those calls are improving. I can say that I had to mature and develop in many ways even after I was considered a "mature" saint.

I was able to glean many nuggets that were instrumental in the maintenance of my peace.

Never once did I see any indication that neither were giving commentary on politics nor anything else. They were always in motion doing something to uplift one another and the respective communities. It was a soothing relationship of mentorship from them both even at a distance. I was able to glean many nuggets that were instrumental in the maintenance of my peace.

Now, I have only met Pastor Charles Heam in person once which was emotional for me because of the powerful anointing resting on him. Our online communication is limited and can be very challenging. But the adage of a picture is worth a thousand words really applies to him.

Am I appearing weak for this transparent account? YES! And the truth did make me free to glean wisdom. So, our discipleship was challenged during this period especially if you are one given to daily rituals. But I thank God for the disruption of the pandemic to force me to reassess my personal dedication and walk. Selah.

CONCLUSION

The pandemic forced many to view and re-view their living conditions as well as companions. Our focus influenced our sight. I tried to focus on as many positive thoughts as I could. Yet, this does not negate the fact that you think, hear, see, and focus on negative things if presented. Media is notorious for seeking ratings, not presenting truth.

I began to reevaluate my home life. Now we were stuck in this dwelling together without the escape of employment, community involvement, CHURCH (did I emphasize church), and a myriad of other welcomed and sought out distractions and escape. While it was a time of frenzied activity to me prior to the full onset of the pandemic, I didn't realize the impact that the near future would hold.

As I stated earlier, I was in Arkansas to commemorate the Day of Remembrance from when the Marshallese people were removed from their land for the United States to test nuclear weapons. The event unleashed shame for my government and how everything happened. Then to top it off, I fell painfully ill and had to rush during the wee hours of the morning to the emergency room. So, there was much that I had going on preceding the actual pandemic. Then the lockdown occurs followed by nonsensical behavior.

We were thrust into the role of community pastors.

But something else occurred as well. We were thrust into the role of *community pastors*. We didn't realize that we were already performing ministry for many that would not even touch the doorknob of a church. While not all people were running from churches, some just couldn't fathom not physically going and speaking to a pastor. Then there were those leaders who just let the church close without any explanation. I was really taken back in discovering scenarios like this! Their congregants gravitated toward anyone that would give them the unadulterated word of God with encouragement in this season.

The building for the church was closed. The Church never closes.

I began reading voraciously while paying close attention to my home life. The major adjustment was that there was no viable and sustained escape. But the major lesson that I learned was that those behaviors that upset you are probably behaviors that you do yourself and give yourself grace. So, flip the script and check your own behaviors.

I gave much thought to those who were alone. I had contact with many people including in person contact within reason. Yet, there were elderly or homebound people that had no contact. We began being their contact, assisting them with whatever was needed. The building for the church was closed. The Church never closes. And we were mobilized like strike troopers.

The community where we reside began bustling with life and concern. Those who may not have come around or spoken to others were now social. There were still those who wished to put a political spin on the events. Yet they were ignored so quickly and completely until many were relegated to standing in lines at stores wreaking havoc. They couldn't do it in the community without repercussions.

It was spectacular viewing the social and spiritual changes occurring in the community.

We were limited as to how far we could go and how long we could be around others. The neighborhood children became friendlier to one another and formed new social groups. Even our pets began to acknowledge one another in different ways. It was spectacular viewing the social and spiritual changes occurring in the community. And during it all, God began rearranging circles and groupings that His people deemed necessary for survival and comfort.

I missed being in church. But I never missed the Word. Our fellowship had prophetically begun preparing well before the pandemic struck. This allowed us to serve the community in ways that no one could have imagined would be needed. It is imperative to be under the capable leadership of a servant of God that hears Him clearly. Essential personnel found it soothing to have a daycare operated by a church at full function even in the pandemic. Too many businesses closed. Yet, because of obedience to God we were in position to be a blessing to many not only in church but outside of the building.

I was always told that chaos means everything is present, but not in order.

Not only was the service broadcast, but one could always go back and review it over and over. (This was the best feature in my opinion!) The church grew during this period! Giving increased. And we continued growing in the Lord. It was phenomenal to see God working in the middle of what many considered chaos. I was always told that chaos means everything is present, but not in order. This was chaos. Everything we needed was present in life. It was just not in order. But under the capable leadership of the current pastor, this transition and disturbance was considered par for the course.

But as promised I will be transparent. My realization was that my "love" for God never changed. However, my practices began displaying the view of ritualistic banter. When I felt empty because I couldn't travel to the building for fellowship, I had to begin searching for my reasons. For this one dilemma I came to the realization that I had allowed ritualistic practice to take over what was once a joyful spiritual discipline. It was like wanting something so bad and then discounting it once you obtained it. I wanted to be in the presence of the Lord among saints so badly until I finally realized that I had become a victim of "Habitual Ritual". God allowed a shift and yet here I was trying to go back to the habitual actions.

Again, I was and still am affected by this pandemic that attacked with such ferocity. Life changed for many and especially me, forever. I witnessed many defying the governmental instructions as an attack on God. I had no idea how anyone could logically say that wearing a mask for safety precautions attacked an omnipotent God!

There was an immediate declaration of rebellion.

At the onset of the pandemic, we were literally standing in a funeral gathering preparing to drive back to our home six states away. Immediately there began declarations of what they were not going to do or not do concerning the governmental instructions. I reminded them of Romans 13:1,2. No thought was even given to the situation at hand. There was an immediate declaration of rebellion. I didn't understand it since the funeral was for their pastor who would not have allowed such declarations.

While I had no problem with the governmental directives, I did have many moments of disdain for religious leaders.

Certainly, many untimely and unnecessary deaths occurred. I don't wish to recap those events again for they are emotionally and spiritually draining. Yet, the observations caused me to regroup personally. While I had no problem with the governmental directives, I did have many moments of disdain for religious leaders. I will take my pause and redirect at this moment to explain my disdain for religious leaders.

The position of pastor is one to lead as a shepherd, not drive like a goat herder.

Recently, I was burdened by the Lord to apply for a position of "part-time pastor". I couldn't make sense of the burden because I had never felt one like that before. As a matter of fact, I never competed for such a position before without being directed to do so. Those who know me know that I don't run toward positions of influence. Let me stay behind the scenes. I know that the position has responsibility connected to it not only for yourself, but responsibility for others as well. The position of pastor is one to lead as a shepherd, not drive like a goat herder. I was given the opportunity to choose whether to continue the process. God showed me various avenues that could be taken along with the outcomes they would follow and left the decision up to me. None of the avenues were comfortable. But the outcome has effects that reach well beyond me. That is what made it so hard.

I do agree that God gives us all strength to accomplish His purposes.

I chose to withdraw my consideration. Why? I made this choice not because of perceived resistance from those who eschewed change or any difficulty. I made it because of the ability to sustain the vision that is given while doing something that many pastors struggle with; family priority. At every venture the cost must be counted, especially if there is a major transition involved. I am confident in my ability to lay the foundation and begin the new work with it being sustained initially. But, because of my age among other factors, I would not be able to logically sustain the work based on my ability alone as no one should. And not to cast any disdain on the church board, but a business model with certain expectations in that situation would not be viable. This is not to mention that I literally "saw" things concerning my family and someone whom I would have leaned heavily on for wisdom. That gentleman transitioned to heaven. This is why God tells us to lean only on Him.

I once had a very prominent pastor tell me that his fear for many decades was that he would be successful at doing something wrong. That stuck with me. Often, we are very successful in doing something apart from what God has desired. This was a fear of mine as well. God's power and might begin at the end of our perceived ability.

I know there will be those who say the Lord will give you strength. I do agree that God gives us all strength to accomplish His purposes. However, He tells us that wisdom is the principal thing. And since I am also understanding, I sought out wise counsel. Ironically what I began to hear in my inner man was only communicated to me by two individuals out of twelve. Everyone else would lend to me thinking that I was to (borrowing a phrase from someone who scared me with their lack of wisdom) "kick down the devil's door and drag him out". Thank God for Joshua and Caleb.

I felt that heaviness knowing that I would not continue with all that could be done.

Ironically, the wise counsel that I sought out was very diverse. Out of twelve people, only two told me that if my spirit was not at peace after the last task given (which was very detailed up to that point) had fully accomplished, then don't continue the process. Ten others gave me the encouraging Christian rehearsed responses of going in to possess the land, getting all that God is giving me and kick down the doors that are cracked. Yet, this didn't resonate in my spirit. Therefore, I withdrew the consideration after ministering my trial sermon where God totally switched the message (and me) at that moment. It was the hardest and most difficult message that I have EVER ministered because I could see in the spirit (which really scared me at times). It was a situation where I was instructed to see it and say it. There was no time for me to allow my own "understanding" to creep into it. My complete body "felt" the spirit realm drain me as I stood. Never let anyone tell you that they are gallivanting in the spirit realm.

With what the trustees desired and what needed to be accomplished both spiritually and socially I could very well have crippled the ministry unintentionally.

I truly felt like Samuel having to follow God while Saul was being disciplined and chastised. I felt that heaviness knowing that I would not continue with all that could be done.

So why did I withdraw consideration? I did so because it would not be feasible to expect me to sustain the momentum under a pastor of my age. With what the trustees desired and what needed to be accomplished both spiritually and socially I could very well have crippled the ministry unintentionally. I do understand the history of Moses and his age. However, that one instance was for Moses. It was not for Ernest. Therefore, setting ego, pride, and anything else that hinders Kingdom expansion aside, I withdrew my consideration and immediately began praying for the congregation.

Many in the Body of Christ will not move to allow progression to any degree. We are not God's only tool! And in an additional display of transparency, I had already begun to fast for direction only for Him to give me the direction totally opposite from what I thought. I was so immersed in past observations of tradition until I felt this was the only move God could make. Imagine that mindset.

It was like the pandemic was a modern-day Tower of Babel.

The impact extended even into avenues of recreation. Where I could go to an arcade with the grandchildren and have a blast, now recreation had to be "adjusted" to allow safety concerns. We began doing more outdoor recreational things like fishing, crabbing and just nature walks. In these activities we encountered many others that we normally may never have connected with. Again, all things worked for His purpose, not ours. It was like the pandemic was a modern-day Tower of Babel. New connections require new languages and places.

The discrepancies of faith began to invade my existence. I became very depressed as I witnessed what was happening not only in my life, but the Body of Christ as well. Christian nationalism began springing up all over. This would be an innocuous phrase if it were taken at face value. However, this term is associated with a racial and bigoted undertone.

While it sounded ultra-righteous and holy it is a bunch of hogwash that needs to be destroyed. I have no understanding of how as citizens, we have so many resources to study, analyze and teach history. I have no clue how someone can not only state this lie but perpetuate it. While not all the United States believes or practices this, there are enough people that truly believe this lie that would attempt to cover up other lies concerning America and her history.

I listened to many declare that they had a "word from the Lord" that none should take precautions.

Clergy began telling people to practice civil disobedience by not masking or being vaccinated. I listened to many declare that they had a "word from the Lord" that none should take precautions. This was just a ploy of the devil using a leftist government according to many. Then their congregants started transitioning to heaven. I do understand civil disobedience having lived through and witnessed the Civil Rights Movement. But, with this I had no idea why this was such a rebellion. I was shocked at how many were in the media speaking of these things like they were the supernatural authority on the pandemic and its direction. As with anything false, it traveled much faster than the truth. And did it ever take off! How is it that the Bible clearly states that we are to obey those in authority and even pray for them so we can live peacefully but the people of God decide to disobey? I have no clue of the reasoning that was provided! Was the truth concerning this relegated to those not in the scientific community but to the social media gurus? Either way I still refused to subscribe to the nonsense I witnessed.

So many "cures" were circulating through social media until fact checking became a necessity for any post concerning the pandemic or the politics surrounding it. While President Donald J. Trump said he was kidding when he suggested drinking bleach, there were those of his followers that tried drinking bleach! I heard so many cures that were utterly ridiculous! But I was surprised at the number of people that placed faith in them. I don't blame them totally. In such times as the pandemic, faith and hope are necessities even if they are askew. We must have some semblance of hope.

> **One individual who is a special needs citizen would always make my day with such enthusiasm and joy making my sandwich.**

Those with professions and assignments considered "lowly" were the main ones that kept society flowing! The migrant workers kept food coming to our stores (so we could have culinary-sanctioned boxing matches while grocery shopping).

I practiced well before the pandemic to treat those in such positions with honor whenever I encountered them. One individual who is a special needs citizen would always make my day with such enthusiasm and joy making my sandwich. I loved waiting in line just for him. When the pandemic was at its pinnacle, he ensured he gave everyone an encouraging word. This deposit in the community should not have been overlooked. But it was.

As I stated earlier, I am being transparent about my struggles through the pandemic and the accompanying difficulties. Yet after going through them and arriving on the other side of "through", I saw what began this quick decline in my spiritual walk. It surely wasn't what I thought would be my struggle. Surely this self-assessed super saint would not have such struggles as maintaining a life of prayer and study of the Word. No. I was only to have struggles in casting out demons and making the earth stand still for twenty-four hours, not with such elementary disciplines as prayer and reading my word! But these were the major struggles that I experienced, personally. I experienced the basics being neglected. And it showed drastically in my life.

I regularly attended many scheduled and even unscheduled services and fellowships.

These two, prayer and studying the Word, were the very first signs of the accelerated and expedited decline of my spiritual discipline. We don't realize when another activity or action will prompt us to perform another activity or action associated with discipline. This was my situation with the onset of COVID-19. I regularly attended many scheduled and even unscheduled services and fellowships. Automatically because of the atmosphere your desire "should" increase to worship, study and grow. However, the pandemic limited my exposure to the "atmosphere" of God and His people. The only people were us. Eventually I stopped "practicing His presence" because I wasn't in His presence with others that I deemed necessary. That's where I cried out to die. It was horrible. I realized at this moment that I was trying to remove my existence from the being of God and live on my own!!! A powerful depression fell upon me. I immediately went into prayer and mourning.

I am certain that I am not the only one that may have felt downtrodden, defeated, or overwhelmed prior to attending a worship experience. I have attended many in this state. And once I attended and joined in the presence of like-minded believers I was exhorted to continue in joy. These times weren't as prevalent now. Even as I write this conclusion, I sadly remember how empty I often felt apart from my brethren. Notice I said I 'felt' empty, not that I was. Again, separation from the flock will allow the enemy to speckle your mind with all types of negative thoughts. If this is continuously allowed some root will form from these thoughts.

My faith was tested in such a way that I began to re-examine myself to see if I was still in the faith! So many saints would just spout off religious platitudes and cliches that were EMPTY. Little cliches filled the air to give the fake fragrance of discount air fresheners mixed with the sour trash fragrance smelling like summer garbage truck juices. In situations like these, I can understand when the Word speaks of being hot or cold. Don't mix anything with your distinction in the Lord. This way when (not if) your faith is tested you will be able to stand completely on faith and not hoping to recapitulate some snazzy cliché to sound spiritual. Sadly, we often don't understand when we accept the Lord's sacrifice for our sins, we still have issues called the vicissitudes of life.

The only other time my faith was tested close to this level is when I was first saved. I was told in an impromptu meeting after church that all my troubles would go away. Everything in my life would be peachy keen! And I happily believed them. I was beyond ready for this! Within the next two weeks I was sent to the Marshall Islands to clean up radioactive debris for nine months. I stayed there three months after the allotted tour. The average temperature seemed hotter than fish grease. Nothing was peachy keen in any way. I felt like I had been deceived into a religious activity that almost destroyed my faith and all desire to push on.

Yet, while on the island I was still searching for those in faith that could help me. In this instance concerning the pandemic, I was one of the ones that people were searching for. It seemed as if going into public was exposing us to many that were looking for hope. My hope is in Christ. So, we gave them our Hope and His identity. So, this pressure was spiritually, socially, and personally induced. I most likely placed more personal pressure on myself than any other contributing source. We are often our own worst enemies and critics.

The greatest loss in the eyes of man is death.

I reiterated my personal humility during this season. I had been faced with multiple close deaths, deaths that could have been avoided and sudden deaths that occurred for various reasons of close relationships. I had personally faced everything that would give me fear. The foundation of all fears is loss. The greatest loss in the eyes of man is death. Therefore, I had to face death in such a way to eliminate all other fears. The enemy will use any type of fear as an antithesis against faith. Therefore, I had to die, again and again and again. It was my responsibility to kill my flesh and get back in unison. I realized that "I" must die again. And God was expecting me to crucify this flesh that allowed me to drift away from the most precious disciplines of my life.

The immediate and sudden onset of death in this situation woke again fears that were all rooted in death. Who would be next? People transitioned from this world to the spirit realm of heaven. I grasped firmly my foundation of faith in Christ as an antithesis of fear while beginning to see all the other entanglements the enemy was shooting at us. As those layers were peeled back, the Lord allowed such peace to come over me while showing me what cracks allowed those seeds to take root.

THIS is where I realized that God was allowing (and requiring) me to kill my own flesh.

Now it was up to me to repair all the cracks, shore up my foundation and to begin helping others. I felt that I shouldn't have had to experience this. But I am the perfect one, so I unconsciously thought. I discovered that flesh does resurrect as well. We must continue a constant circumcision of the heart while simultaneously and continuously crucifying the flesh.

THIS is where I realized that God was allowing (and requiring) me to kill my own flesh. I was to kill what was becoming "myself" to return to Him. And

I welcomed it. This complete ordeal happened unexpectedly "Once Upon a Time Called COVID".

www.ingramcontent.com/pod-product-compliance
Lightning Source LLC
Chambersburg PA
CBHW050327010526
44119CB00050B/711